The Trail to Santa Fe:
A Pilgrim's Progress

Willard H. Smith
An Autobiography

Willard H. Smith

Published by the author
Goshen College, Goshen, Indiana 46526
1985

Printed at Evangel Press, Nappanee, Indiana
46550-0189.

To Verna
My beloved companion, who faithfully, loyally and devotedly traveled most of the trail with me.

Contents

Preface (Warning) 1

Acknowledgement and Credits 3

1. Beginnings 5

2. Grade School Years 17

3. Interlude 1915-1917 35

4. The Hesston Years
1917-1921 45

5. Detour 1921-1926 59

6. Completing College: Goshen 1926-1928 69

7. Ann Arbor 1928-1929 75

8. A Pup Instructor at Goshen College /
University of Chicago 1929-1935 83

9. Completing Graduate Work: Indiana
University 1935-1937 103

10. Return to Goshen 1937-1943 111

11. "Paraguayan Interlude" 1944-1945 131

12. The Post-War Years 1946-1954 149

13. Another Interlude — Mexico 1954-1955 169

14. Fulfilling Years 1955-1968 177

15. Toward Retirement 1968 — 191

16. End of the Trail: Going Home 209

Preface (Warning)

This book is my autobiography—my *me*moirs, as Will Rogers used to say. I call it my fun writing. One reason I am having fun writing it is because, unlike most of my writing, I am not much concerned about documentation and footnotes. I am getting the material out of thin air—in other words, my head. So I am calling this preface a warning: a warning to the reader that not every statement in this book may reach the high standard of gospel truth. In his later years, Mark Twain once said something to the effect that when he was young he could remember everything, whether it happened or not; but now that he was old he could remember only the latter (the things that hadn't happened!). So let the reader beware!

But that does not mean there is no information in this volume. Again, I have to think of Mark Twain who wrote in his preface to *Roughing It*:

"Yes, take it all around, there is quite a good deal of information in the book. I regret this very much, but really it could not be helped: information appears to stew out of me naturally, like the precious ottar of roses out of the otter." He wished he could retain his facts, but he could not. "The more I calk up the sources, and the tighter I get, the more I leak wisdom. Therefore, I can only claim indulgence at the hands of the reader, not justification." More seriously, while neither Verna (my wife) nor I kept diaries—except for a few days on rare occasions—there are available other aids to memory: such as letters, memo books, speeches, clippings, pictures, persons who participated in the events I write about, especially family members, and particularly my beloved companion who traveled most of the trail with me. In fact, it is in part a narrative of her pilgrimage too—hence the frequent use of the word "we". In so many cases the experiences were shared ones.

1

Perhaps I should clarify the title. In part it is a takeoff from my interest in western history, with a slant toward the southwest and its Spanish connections. Santa Fe, of course, means "Holy Faith." So the title, with subtitle, covers my pilgrimage, spiritual and otherwise. I should also warn the reader that there is a good deal in the book about our travels, especially after we retired in 1972 when we had more time for that. But even before we retired we traveled a lot because we strongly believed in its educational value. With the exception of the case I mention in Chapter 2, when I was only thirteen years of age and too young to appreciate the beauties of Colorado, I cannot think of a single instance where I took a trip and then regretted it. There are some I contemplated and now regret I did not take them.

In Chapter 16, which of course is anticipatory, I give my views of what faces the Christian pilgrim at the end of the trail.

Various members of my family have read the manuscript and made suggestions. My sister Dorothy Smith Shank and Helen Wade Alderfer gave the work a special reading. I thank all the readers for their suggestions, many of which I have accepted. Also I thank Ron Gunden and his staff in College Relations, and Stuart Showalter and his staff in Information Services, especially, Karen Hirschy, Rachel Miller Ulrich, Cindy Hawkins, and Myrna Kaufman for typing the manuscript and putting it on the word processor. Terry Stutzman, assisted by Suelyn Lee, did excellent work in designing, pasting up, and performing other detailed labors in getting the work ready for printing by the Evangel Press in Nappanee, Indiana.

Willard H. Smith
Professor Emeritus of History
Goshen College, Goshen, Indiana
July 1985

Acknowledgment and Credits

To Doubleday and Company, Inc., Garden City, New York, for the quote (page 220) from Bruce Catton's book, *Waiting for the Morning Train: An American Boyhood,* pp. 252-53.

To Northern Michigan University Press, Marquette, Michigan, for quotes (page 79) from Dwight L. Dumond's book, *America's Shame and Redemption,* pp.170-71.

To Lillian Eichler Watson and *Greencroft Courier,* 1977, for her remarks about and quote from Sir William Mulock, as given on pages 218-19 of my book.

To *The Elkhart Truth,* Elkhart, Indiana, for the picture of Carl Sandburg and myself, 1953.

CHAPTER 1
Beginnings

The trail began four miles northeast of Eureka, Illinois, and four and a half miles southwest of Roanoke. On October 15, 1900, I was born on a farm a half-mile south of the Roanoke Amish-Mennonite church, as it was then called. My parents were John J. and Katie E. (Smith) Smith. Unfortunately, I cannot trace my ancestry back very far. Mother's father was Bishop John Smith, whose father, Christian Smith (Schmidt), came from Lorraine France to Pennsylvania in 1829, and in 1833 to the Partridge Creek settlement near the present Metamora. Grandfather Smith married Magdalena Schertz, sister of the minister Peter D., which relates us to one of the large Schertz tribes in that area. Magdalena's father was David Schertz and her mother was a Bachman. Bishop John Smith's father, Christian, married Catherine Bechler, whose parents were Jacob Bechler and Anna Gerber Bechler.

On father's side the family line to the intelligible past is equally short. Grandfather Peter Smith married Barbara Neuhauser, the daughter of Peter Neuhauser and Mary Schmitt Neuhauser. Peter was the son of Jacob Neuhauser and Catherine Sommers Neuhauser, and Mary was the daughter of Jacob Peter-Schmitt and Barbara Lauber Peter-Schmitt.

Nearly if not all the above mentioned great-grandparents and great-great-grandparents were from Alsace-Lorraine, France. Uncle C. Henry Smith made various efforts to secure more information about our family history. He was not successful in gleaning a great deal of information. But he did state that probably the Smiths on both my father's and mother's side go back not too far—to the same person. Information

5

from various sources, including Aunt Mary Imhoff (Mrs. Christian H. Smith's mother), supported the validity of the story. Considerable evidence indicates that my great-great-grandfather on mother's side, Christian Schmidt, was killed in a mill at Guermange near Metz, Lorraine. Likely either his father or grandfather was the ancestor for both lines of Schmidts. That would have made my father and mother third or fourth cousins (or third cousins "once improved"!).

Though my forebears came to America from Alsace-Lorraine in the first part of the nineteenth century, they originated in Switzerland and like other Amish and Mennonites left that country because of persecution. So far as I know my ancestors in Alsace-Lorraine all followed Jacob Ammann in his dispute with the Mennonites in the 1690s. This meant that they became quite strict in dress and social customs and in the interpretation of scriptures relating to taking communion with church members against whom discipline had been exercised because of sin in their lives and who thus were not in fellowship with the church. Ammann's followers (Amish) applied I Corinthians 5:11—"not to eat" or "not to keep company" with backsliders—to mean the natural table as well as the communion table, whereas the Mennonites applied these phrases only to the communion table. But the Amish who came to Illinois in the nineteenth century, while continuing to discipline and if necessary excommunicate sinning church members, soon gave up the idea of ostracizing them socially.

By 1900 when I was born most of the Amish had become known as Amish Mennonites. This is of course what they were all along, but earlier they were usually referred to as Amish. But in Illinois they were quite different in 1900 from what they were when they started arriving in the 1830s. They were beginning to use

English more and German less in their homes and church services, buttons had replaced hooks and eyes in their dress, and in other ways also their life style had become less separatist and exclusive. On the main issue which had brought about separation from the Mennonites in the 1690s—socially shunning or ostracizing backsliding members—the Amish Mennonites had accepted the softer Mennonite interpretation and position. Significantly, unlike the changes in some states, all of these changes in Illinois occurred without a group pulling off from the main body and developing what became known as the Old Order Amish. The Old Order Amish which exist today in the Arthur area have no connection with the central Illinois Amish. They migrated largely from eastern United States after the Civil War.

Yet one cannot say that all of these central Illinois Amish moved along together in their changes and adjustments to new conditions. One group followed Henry Egly, an Indiana Amish leader who felt that the Amish were not sufficiently emphasizing the new birth and personal experience of salvation. In 1865 he started a new denomination which became known as the Defenseless Mennonites and later as the Evangelical Mennonite Church. Some of the Illinois Amish Mennonites joined this body. In the 1870s a still larger group followed Joseph Stuckey, a progressive leader from Danvers, Illinois. While more liberal or progressive in their religious outlook they retained enough of the old beliefs that for years they were called "Stuckey Amish." Later they organized the Central Conference Mennonite Church and in the 1950s became a part of the General Conference Mennonites.

My family was a part of the larger group which became known as Amish Mennonites. In the 1880s the Illinois Amish Mennonites, along with those of the states west of the Mississippi River, formed the Western District Amish Mennonite Conference. This continued until 1920 when the Illinois Amish Mennonites and the (Old) Mennonites formed the present Illinois Mennonite Conference.

It was in this Amish Mennonite home that I lived a sheltered, secure, happy life. In due course three brothers and a sister came along to make life still more exciting and pleasant—Tilman, Milton, Dorothy, and George. Blessed with loving, devoted, Christian parents, we felt a security and level of wealth—in terms of meeting our needs—far above our modest economic level.

As to my earliest remembrances in our home I cannot claim much precocity. I can remember things, but I cannot say exactly how young or old I was. I remember going to the kitchen window where, by standing on my tip-toes, I could look out into the yard and barnyard and see what was going on. But that means little in terms of my age because I do not know how high the window sills were from the floor! One fond memory is that of baking day (Saturday?), when mother baked pies and other things and with left-over dough made cinnamon rolls for us youngsters. She no doubt planned to have some extra dough for the purpose. We always looked forward with high anticipation to the hour when she would call us to the cinnamon-roll lunch! But again I cannot pinpoint how old I was when these delightful episodes occurred.

Nor can I remember when I got the few spankings I received. Oh yes, I remember the occasions, but not how old I was. One time, soon after getting lightning rods on our buildings—probably somewhere around the period of 1906 to 1908—I was messing around with one of the ground wires, pulling it out of the ground a bit. Later dad asked me some embarrassing questions about it, in answering which I was not as forthright as I should have been. When he asked whether I pulled up the wire, I neither admitted nor clearly denied it, but said I saw Tim there and maybe he did it. This answer far from satisfied father. Pretty soon I found myself "dancing" to the tune of the hickory stick (or peach limb or whatever) in the old smokehouse. Suffice it to say that a lesson in honesty, though sternly administered, was strongly implanted on my soul as well as my rear! We grow through experience and such lessons in early life were of tremendous help to all of us children later in life, for which I have been eternally grateful.

One early reminiscence I can date a bit more closely. It was probably early in 1906, when I was five, that Grandpa (Bishop John) Smith presented us boys with a little wooden farm wagon. Since he died July 6, 1906, he probably gave us the wagon not more than a few weeks or months before. As stated earler, Grandpa Smith was the only grandparent we children saw; hence the gift, which we prized most highly, helped endear him to us as a revered, kindly, loving forebear. His son, C. Henry Smith, also knew how to ingratiate himself with his nephews and nieces. His many gifts to us over the years, beginning with pencils, pencil boxes, and crayons in preschool days, made lasting impressions upon us. This is not to say of course that these were the only relatives who favored us with gifts.

There were many other childhood memories, some of which go back to preschool days. One form of entertainment for us kids was to hitch old Doll to a pre-plumbing tin bathtub and have her—with her granddaughter colt beside her—drag us down the road for an afternoon joy ride. The colt was very tame. We had learned how to make it so by feeding it sugar. But I learned the hard way that even a tame colt can kick like blazes when surprised. One day while "riding," the bath tub hit the rear legs of the colt. Instinctively the animal fired away, and since I was in the front "seat" I got the full impact of the blow in my chest. I as well as the colt was surprised, and it took me a moment or two to recover my wind, not to say my self-esteem.

It must have been very early when I tried to follow in dad's footsteps when he was working around home and when I would serve as his errand boy. Frequently he would have me run after something—a wrench or a hammer in the shop or something else—then he would add, "See how fast you can run." Dad knew how to get action out of me for I would run like Jehu to meet his challenge!

Another highlight that went back to early days was the exchange of visits with the King relatives in Kansas at Hesston and Hutchinson. The Kings had moved to Kansas from Illinois in 1885 and father, whose parents had died before this, went with them. He lived there with or near the Kings for some four or five years before returning to Illinois. Both Mrs. Samuel B. King (Anna) and Mrs. Emmanuel J. King (Lena) were father's sisters. While father was the youngest of six children (three sisters and three brothers), and thus felt keenly the early loss of his parents, all were young enough to have felt a close family tie because of common experience. This closeness remained throughout their lives, which bond was strengthened by fairly frequent exchanges of visits with the Kansas relatives. One of my prized possessions is a songbook (*Crowning Day No. 6*) which has on the flyleaf this inscription by mother: "J. J. Smith. This was written in the Pennsylvania meetinghouse [this was the name of the Mennonite meetinghouse then located between Newton and Hesston] while waiting for Bible Reading to started [sic]. Newton Kansas." Unfortunately the statement is undated. But it was very likely written within a few years after 1904, the date when the songbook was copyrighted and published. Both father and mother had good voices and sang considerably. I remember dad's singing more than mother's. Father did a great deal of singing in the home, especially while rocking the children to sleep in the evening. For many years he also served as chorister in Sunday school and church services. I remember one time as a small youngster how embarrassed I was when he announced a song by its title, "Stand Up for Jesus." I thought he meant we should literally stand up for Jesus, which I did, but was embarrassed when I stood there alone. I sat down forthwith.

Not only did father like singing; he must have had some interest also in instrumental music. In any case he owned a violin or "fiddle," which he kept on top of the kitchen cupboard. Quite often after work in the evening he would get down the fiddle and play us some tunes, some serious and some not so serious.

This kitchen cupboard was famous for something else. Another early memory recalls the fact that dad used the top of the cupboard for storing his cigars which he occasionally smoked. The use of tobacco in some form was not uncommon among Amish Mennonites in those days. Some of my uncles chewed the weed, and continued to do so long after dad terminated his brief period of occasional smoking in the house. One evening, according to Tim's recollection, dad got down a cigar and told mother that this was the last one he was going to smoke. The boys were growing up and he was going to quit. No doubt his leadership in church and Sunday school helped influence his decision, plus the fact that his father-in-law, Bishop John Smith, had been speaking against the use of liquor and tobacco for years. So far as I know dad kept his promise.

As I wrote earlier, I knew only one of my grand-parents—mother's father, John Smith. But even he was taken when I was only five years old. His first wife died in 1898 and he married a widow, Lydia Albrecht Slagel, over a year and a half later. Grandfather's funeral in July, 1906, made an impression on me and I remember it well. The fact that one of his sisters and her family, the Joe Lehmans who were neighbors, could come to the home but could not attend the funeral service at home or at the Roanoke Church because of their membership in the exclusive Apostolic Christian Church caused numerous remarks.

According to the *Metamora Herald*, the funeral and the funeral procession were the "Largest ever seen in [the] county." One small, unimportant incident in the funeral procession made a big impression on my young mind. Enroute my brother Tim had to go to the toilet. It happened while passing the home of Uncle Peter D. Schertz. So father pulled out of the procession and into the home for a brief "rest" stop. Upon resuming the journey father took a different route for a few miles and drove more rapidly in order to take our proper place again with the family near the head of the procession. Throughout this entire episode I worried unduly about not making it, and I think I even wondered why my (three-year-old) brother could not train his bowels to be a little more regular and not cause our family such embarrassment! But after rejoining the procession, it proceeded without further incident to the Roanoke meetinghouse, where grandfather had been minister and bishop. Two prominent fellow Amish Mennonite bishops, Samuel Gerber of Groveland, Illinois, and Sebastian Gerig of Wayland, Iowa, had charge of the services.

After grandfather had gone life of course was not the same. But grandmother and the other members of the

12

family carried on bravely. About this time Agnes began to keep a diary and left us an invaluable record. She and her mother, Lydia Smith, (our step-grandmother) were much interested in the work of the church and attended many of its meetings. Agnes's diary reports are therefore valuable for reporting family matters as well as the larger church activities. Until Agnes married Chris J. Gunden and moved to Flanagan, she and grandmother continued to live in the home which grandfather had built a bit west of the old home place when he married the second time.

Though Grandfather Smith was now gone, another grandpa tended to take his place. Christian S. Schertz—no blood relative—was the father of our Uncle Ben and lived directly across the road from us. Ben had married my mother's sister, Emma, and lived next to his parents. Both families were very close to us, not only geographically but in other ways also. In 1875 Grandpa Schertz had given land from his farm for the Roanoke meetinghouse and was later ordained minister in this congregation. His wife, Phoebe, a kindly "grandmother" to us, went to her reward long before he did.

One early reminiscence illustrates the grandfatherly concern which Grandpa Schertz had for us children. One summer evening after the day's work, the hired hand, who was in his late teens or early twenties, and some of us older children were out on the road playing "horse." I was trying to drive the "horse" which was balky. During this frustrating experience I used some very strong language that I had not learned in Sunday school. Lo and behold, the next day grandpa had a chat with me in which he disclosed the embarrassing news that he had heard my profanity the night before! But he was kind and reassuring. He admonished me how bad it was to use profanity and added he would not tell my father about this if I promised not to use such language in the future. It was not difficult to persuade me to accept this bargain, and I readily did so.

Too readily, I'm afraid, for I did not keep the promise fully, though it might have helped some. A few years later, after I was driving real horses—and I started very early, probably at about eight or nine years of age—I had another embarrassing experience about flying off the handle and using language that neither grandpa nor my parents had taught me. One summer night during oats harvest I started dreaming and recapitulated the events of the day before. I had been driving a three- or-four horse team on a binder, and I felt their performance merited the use of strong language! Father had not heard me during the day, but unfortunately, or fortunately, he heard the repeat performance during the night. (I was sleeping in the same room with him.) He confronted me with the evidence the next morning, and, because of the nature of the case, I was unable to say that I had not used the language. Just as God uses "mysterious ways His wonders to perform," He uses various ways of calling sinners to righteousness!

Where did we learn such language, living as we did in a conservative, protected, rural community? In fact where did we learn other forms of evil in addition to profanity? I regret to say that we were not always models of virtue in some other respects as well. Father tried to have hired men who would exert a good influence on us children. He was almost completely successful in this, but there were a very few exceptions. This is not to suggest however that but for these few exceptions we would have been saintly children. Evil influences come from strange places and cause one to ponder about "original sin."

My reminiscenses of our hired men and women, whether Mennonite or non-Mennonite, are largely positive. Two of our hired girls, Anna and Katie Eberle from west of Washington, were Catholic and served us very acceptably—Anna for at least five years and Katie at least two. One fond memory is that of a visit in the Eberle home, with old Doll hitched to the buggy doing the honors on this fairly long journey.

The world of a rural midwestern boy seventy-five years ago also had its share of tramps, bums, and hoboes—Jim Day, Bill Shuck, Dan Augsburger, Abe O'Larnick. There may be technical differences between these three, but I shall not dwell on that here. Some of them were luckless vagrants who had difficulty in finding and holding a job, but most of them, having constitutional and religious convictions against working, were fearful they might find one. This reminds me of a cartoon I once saw. One sunny morning in late spring two bums who had been walking along a railroad track decided to rest from their weary "labors" and lay down on the sunny side of the railroad embankment. Philosophizing about life, they were discussing how life had treated them. One had found life rather rough and the people not very courteous. The other replied: "Well, life has been good to me. One time in Pittsburgh I was offered a good job, but other than that I have met with nothing but courtesy and kindness." These characters knew where they could find "courtesy and kindness" as well as good Mennonite cooking! In any case we children were always glad to see our ordinary routine changed by the visits and repetitious stories of these men. In a different category, country peddlers also added a bit of excitement to our prosaic lives. One-legged Abe O'Larnick was a good example of this type of itinerant. He too knew where to find good Mennonite cooking and lodging.

CHAPTER 2
Grade School Years

A decent regard for the truth compels me to admit that I did not like school at first. Starting to school was an ordeal that brought tears of protest. I am not even sure which school I first attended, although it was probably the Reeser school which was in our district, one mile and a quarter west of the Roanoke Church. The Schertz school, which I attended some before moving to that district, was a mile east of the Roanoke Church. My cousins, children of Uncle Chris and Aunt Mary Smith, were our neighbors but lived in the Schertz school district. I remember attending that school with them for short periods, probably because I could ride with them. But most of the early memories I have are of the Reeser school.

The time I began was in September 1906. I was only five at the time but turned six in October. The distance to school by the road was a little over one and three-quarters miles, but less when we walked across the fields. How old we were when we started driving faithful old Doll or the younger Mack I do not remember. School patrons had the privilege of building a small barn or shed at the school for their pony or horse, and we had such a facility.

The population of the school district was almost wholly Amish Mennonite or Apostolic Christian—"New Amish" they were often called because of their close connection from the time of their origins in Switzerland in the 1830s. A bit of rivalry between the two groups surfaced occasionally, but on the whole they played and "studied" well together.

How deeply and seriously we studied might be open to question. One of my strongest recollections is the

17

high priority we put on the recess and noon periods when we could get out and play. In winter ice-skating was the highly-prized activity. Skating opportunities were often quite meager; so any little frozen pond and/or ditch along the roadside were used. Our academic priorities were so high that we even used ingenious methods of cutting short the noon lunch period in order to have more time for play. We kept our lunches in our desks where the books were stored. A short time before the lunch hour we frequently engaged in a "diligent search" for this or that book or notepad which failed to appear because the lunch bag was always in the way. So what was left to do but to take a surreptitious bite every now and then? It thus so happened that by the time the lunch hour arrived the food had disappeared and the entire noon period could be used for unadulterated academic activity such as skating or what have you.

How long the teacher permitted this to go on I do not remember. But it did go on, and I was one of those guilty. And what relation if any this had with the following incident I likewise do not recall. One day when it was a little cool in the schoolroom I tied a handkerchief around my head and then asked the teacher whether I could go to the stove to warm up. As I approached the stove she met me with a yardstick in her hands and proceded to inflict some corporal punishment on my rear. It was a moderate spanking and did not last long, for the yardstick was soon in pieces. In addition, according to Tim, one of the fascinated spectators, the teacher got her yardstick tangled up in some strings of beaded popcorn on a nearby Christmas tree, with the corn of course flying in every direction. I am not sure what led up to all this, but I must have been "showing off" a bit more than what the temperature really warranted.

I remember too a few—very few—attempts at writing poetry. One day after Thanksgiving teacher had us write short poems on that subject. I don't have the faintest idea what I wrote, but I do remember the Shakespearean effort of Annie Reeser:

Jingle, jingle, jingle,
Pockets full of cash.
Today we eat turkey,
Tomorrow may be hash.

The standing of English grammar as a subject for study, especially during one year of my recollection, was not high. Some few years before I was an eighth-grader I recall the pupils of that grade making such a fuss about the time they were wasting in studying that subject further. They argued with the teacher that as farmers they needed more arithmetic than grammar and succeeded in talking her into letting them substitute an extra arithmetic period in the place of the grammar slot!

The famous McGuffey readers had disappeared in our area by the time I attended school. Cyr's readers had replaced them. But they too had a considerable number of stories which contained the old-fashioned morality. However they apparently were not successful in making a pacifist out of me. One of the few grade books I retained was my *Cyr's Fourth Reader*. Probably the chief reason I still have it is the autograph and the statement I wrote on the fly-leaf: "Don't steel [sic] this book, for the owner carries a revolver with him." My pacifist ideas came later! According to the date of the autograph, I still had time to develop them.

Friday afternoons usually brought a welcome change in the school routine, the last hour or two before closing often being devoted to a spelling bee, ciphering match, or similar activity. Occasionally this involved a contest with a nearby school. Our outstanding master in ciphering in the Reeser school was Johnnie Rocke. Whenever we had ciphering contests, whether at home or elsewhere, we could depend on Johnnie winning hands down. He was a whiz!

One exciting change in the routine during my grade school days was an extended visit to Texas, which our family made during the winter of 1908-1909. According to a letter written by mother enroute, we must have left Eureka about or before December 15, and returned probably some time in February. After visiting relatives and friends in Newton, Hutchinson, Larned and Harper, Kansas, and Medford, Oklahoma, we arrived in Tuleta, Texas, on or about December 28. Since I visited Medford only once, but visited the Kansas points—especially Newton where Uncle Sam Kings lived and Hutchinson where Uncle Man Kings resided—on various occasions, I can more easily sort out and associate the happenings at Medford with this journey than I can those that occurred in Kansas. Mother wrote in her letter that ''Willard has a pretty bad cough.'' She put it mildly. I remember it distinctly. I had what they used to call the croup. To make matters worse, I had to sleep with an elderly gentleman, my mother's uncle John Sommer who was also visiting the John and Lena Wagner family. Lena was Sommer's daughter and thus a first cousin of mother. But the relationship didn't help much. Sommer made it clear that he was not too sympathetic with his young, upstart grandnephew who was coughing and whooping in bed with him and disturbing his sleep. So I suffered not only from coughing, but even more so from disturbing my great-uncle's nocturnal peace and peaceful disposition.

This trip to Texas was an eye-opener to me. We remained in Tuleta long enough for me to enroll in school, but I remember nothing I learned from there.

This was a case however where traveling was really educational. Enroute from Medford I remember especially Ft. Worth, Texas, a center on the Santa Fe railway where I saw many trains, tracks, and my first sight of locomotives using oil instead of coal. I was fascinated also by the large number of Blacks we saw and also by the increasing number of Mexicans or Spanish Americans we encountered as we moved toward the gulf coast.

One incident on the train was more embarrassing at that time than it would have been today. Milt, who was a bit less than three years old, got a hold of my cap and tossed it across the coach. Since the weather was warm and the windows open, my cap went right on out! This produced a crisis of the first magnitude in my young mind! I thought the proper solution of the crisis was to stop the train, back up, and recover the precious cap. But no one, least of all the train officials, agreed with me. So we had to make some embarrassing shifts in the family wardrobe until we were able to stop and buy a new cap. I wore Tims's cap, Tim wore Milt's and Milt had to get along with a scarf or handkerchief tied around his head.

Living in Tuleta likewise had its educational features. Tuleta was a small, sleepy hamlet with barely a hundred people, located some seventy miles north of Corpus Christi. Tuleta was the center of a small, young Mennonite community, with the starting of which Peter Unzicker, Mennonite minister from Cullom, Illinois, had much to do. We lived in one of his houses. It wasn't the kind to write home about—you could stand on one side and through the cracks see daylight on the other—but how could you be critical about a rent-free house? Uncle Sam Smith, whose wife had recently died, also lived with us. Not many Mennonites resided in the town. As farmers they lived in the surrounding area. We had church services in a schoolhouse just outside the town. Unzicker served as our minister. I remember only a few names of the Mennonites living there at that time: Unzicker, Steiner, King, Teuscher, Kauffman. Ben Litwiller from Hopedale, Illinois, was also there for the winter, along with his sister and her daughter.

The most fascinating residents to me were the Mexicans, or Spanish Americans. This was my introduction to these often-neglected and misunderstood people and the beginning of a contact and interest that have continued to the present. Many of them of course were Mexicans or children of Mexicans—for they immigrated in large numbers after the turn of the century. But as I was to learn later, quite a few of these Spanish Americans were more native Texans and more "American" than the Anglos in that they were descendants of people (Spanish and Indian mixture) who were in Texas long before the Anglos started coming in the 1820s.

The weather in south Texas was delightfully warm, only occasionally when a norther blew down its cold blasts did we suffer the wintry air. Then, especially in our shack-house, we made ingenious efforts to keep warm, including placing carpet strips over the cracks and going to bed with all the clothes we could acquire.

The winter passed all too quickly, and soon we were back in good old Illinois where we again mingled with our relatives and other friends telling them about the strange world of south Texas. The visits with cousins particularly were highlights. Uncle Ben and Aunt Emma Schertz lived almost directly across the road from us. Unfortunately their only daughter, Ruth, was taken by death early in life. Uncle Chris and Aunt Mary Smith with Ed, Martha, Lulu and the younger children also lived nearby. We (especially the cousins) exchanged informal visits frequently. One day I mailed a card to Ed asking him to come over and visit me that afternoon, little realizing that he would not receive the card for a day or two. Thanks to Ed's greater sense of the importance of preserving "valuable historic documents," he recently showed me this and other cards that I had sent him many years ago.

We exchanged highly prized visits with other cousins farther away, although of course not so frequently as with those close by. Since we were all farmers much of our conversation—though not all of it—had to do with farming and our exploits in learning at a very youthful age how to drive a four-horse team pulling this or that piece of farm machinery. I must have had a reputation for precocity in this as I recall the pride I felt when I heard my elders speak with amazement about my achievements in this regard.

Early in 1911 we moved a mile east to a farm which father bought at the unheard-of price of $250 per acre. This put us in the Schertz school district, living one-half mile south of that school. We appreciated the convenience of living much closer to school. Another interesting experience in the same year was the arrival of a sister, a welcome event after the birth of three boys, even though I used language which might have indicated some doubt as to how thrilled I really was by Dorothy's arrival. When uncle Joe Smiths visited us in their new Buick soon after her birth, the first question I asked them was: "Well, do you want to come in and see the little mule?" Since that time I have been spending a great deal of time trying to explain to Dot that that was an inelegant, smart-aleck remark which had nothing to do with indicating my real love and affection for her. After some years I think I fairly well succeeded.

Another big event in our lives was going to Roanoke to see our first airplane. It was about 1911 or 1912. The machine was a small one-motor, one-seater biplane. We paid the grand sum of 10 cents to see this modern miracle. After showing the plane for a time, the pilot took a short flight and proved to the incredulous crowd that this creature actually could get off the ground and remain aloft for some time. We drove home believing we had seen the eighth wonder of the world.

It must have been about 1912 when I reached an important mile-post in my "trail to Santa Fe" (Holy Faith). My recollection is that I was eleven years old when I publicly confessed Christ as my savior and lord and joined the Roanoke Amish Mennonite Church. I did not have an Apostle Paul-Damascus-road experience. But through Christian nurture in the home and church I concluded that I had reached the age of accountablity and responsibility and should make my decision public. We had revival and evangelistic meetings at that time, but I can't remember for certain who the evangelist was when I took this step. Andrew Schrock of Metamora was our bishop, and I remember the instruction class for the converts preceding our baptism.

Along with the sunshine, the years 1912 to 1914 had some deep shadows for our family. Mother became ill with "consumption," as tuberculosis was called in those days. Father did all that loving hands could to restore her to health. Mother spent part of 1912 and 1913 at the Ottawa (Illinois) Tent Colony where the doctors were supposed to be specialists in the treatment of this disease. We all felt the loneliness caused by mother's absence, and mother felt the loneliness of separation even more. Father took us to visit mother as often as possible. I remember riding part of the way in the caboose of a Santa Fe freight train. At times also

Uncle Ben (Schertz) would take us up in his car. (We did not have a car until the end of 1913).

Angels of mercy, in the form of father's nieces from Kansas, came to help us during this difficult year. Grace King from Hesston, and Bertha King from Hutchinson for a shorter period, did an excellent job of taking over the household. Irene Neuhauser from Harper, Kansas, also assisted for a short time.

After about six months at Ottawa Mother came home little improved if any. In that period doctors were emphasizing the importance of the western mountain states in helping to cure various pulmonary and respiratory ailments. So father and mother decided to move the family temporarily to La Junta, Colorado, where the Mennonite Church had constructed a sanitarium a few years before. Father took mother out in December 1913. He then returned home, had an auction sale early in January 1914, and moved to La Junta shortly thereafter. Sister Dorothy, who was a bit over two years of age, remained with Aunt Emma (Mrs. Ben) Schertz.

Located about five miles west of La Junta, the sanitarium was situated on a large farm which the administration operated for the benefit of the institution. Father had been asked to head the farm operations. We lived in a commodious brick house erected very close to the sanitarium. This made it convenient for visiting mother. For the first month or six weeks mother seemed to make fairly good progress. But in February she took a turn for the worse, and her decline was quite rapid. She died March 19, 1914. This was the first break in our family circle and was a traumatic experience for all of us. The real facts surrounding her passing still remain puzzling. Unofficial reports came to the family that a patient, who visited mother more than she probably should have, visited her even after she had contracted spinal meningitis, thus supposedly giving it to mother.

Losing our beloved mother made an indelible impression upon us. I shall never forget the last viewing of her body at the mortuary in La Junta. We children did not go along with father to Illinois where services were held in the Roanoke Mennonite Church. She was laid to rest in the nearby cemetery. Father had asked Allen H. Erb, Mennonite minister from McPherson, **Kansas**, to preach the funeral sermon. I have often wondered why father asked Erb to come from Kansas to perform this service, for the latter became more widely known and influential after 1914. But father earlier must have gotten acquainted with him during visits to Hesston and the Pennsylvania Church where Allen grew up.

The La Junta interlude was an important one for our family. It required considerable adjusting in addition to mother's passing. The irrigation farming in the Arkansas Valley was new to father. But a capable Spanish American hired man, who spent virtually all of his time in irrigating, was the solution to this problem. Joe Mestas and his family became our good friends and felt disappointed later if we visited La Junta and failed to include them in our visits. Joe had boys our ages and we went to school together. When we started to school in Swink—about a mile and a quarter north of us—Milton began to cry. But one of the Mestas boys about his age put his arms around Milton and calmed his fears. Mother reported in a letter that Milton was "alright in a little bit" and added: "Now that was the love of a little Mexican. He thinks a great deal of him and . . . is his chum." There were other Spanish Americans in the community, and it was my second and more important contact with these interesting people. Some of them, in addition to Mestas, worked for us.

Raising new crops such as sugar beets, cantaloupes, and alfalfa was also a part of the readjustment. Operating buckrakes or push-rakes and hay stackers right in the alfalfa fields was also a new experience for me. Our barn was only a shack containing a few horses and had no room for the storing of hay. The poor milk cows had to be "contented" with being tied on the "warm side" of a barbed-wire fence for milking purposes. (An adequate barn was built later.)

The cantaloupes mentioned above were the famous Rocky Ford variety, having been originated in that community and taking their name from the nearby town of that name. About that same time our neighbor, Ed Gauger, living a little over a mile from us, was working on a new variety to be produced shortly and to become still more famous—the Honeydew melon. However, a Mr. Bolles of the area also claimed some credit for developing this variety.

One other feature in Colorado farming that was new to us was the branding of cattle. This tenderfoot from Illinois remembers with horror the suffering he shared with the cattle, especially the calves, as the red-hot irons burned their flesh! It was difficult to explain to the beasts that this treatment was for their own good!

One of the pluses in living at La Junta was the meeting of many new people and the forming of new friendships, some of which have continued to the present. The Ebersoles, Heatwoles, Hersheys, Rhodes, Wineys, Weavers, Stalters, Nunemakers, and Rebers are some names that come readily to mind. Some residents resided there for short periods. One of these families was the T. K. Hersheys, who lived and worked with us at the sanitarium farm. They were young city missionaries who later spent many years as missionaries in Argentina.

Another plus was visiting the mountain areas west of La Junta. I had often heard, read, and studied about the Rocky Mountains. From La Junta one could see the higher peaks on a sunny, clear day. So we looked forward to visiting the Colorado Springs area in early June in our car. Uncle Bens, who remained with us for some months after mother's passing, would go along, but we could not all go at the same time. So Uncle Ben, Keturah Kauffman who worked for us, Emma Eby, head nurse at the sanitarium, Tim, and I constituted the first group. (Miss Eby later became the wife of Dr. Charles Hershey, son of the sanitarium administrator, Jacob M. Hershey. Keturah later married a Mr. Dreier at Hesston, and after his death married Bishop Earl Buckwalter of the same place.) We visited the usual tourist attractions, including Cave of the Winds, Seven Falls, Garden of the Gods, Pikes Peak and historic Cripple Creek. As to Pikes Peak, we thought we would be smart and save money. We started walking up the cog railroad. But by the time we arrived at the halfway station (which was actually less than halfway) we were pretty well exhausted, and decided to take the train for the balance of the journey up and down. Did we ever save money! Instead of the usual $5.00 for the round trip we paid only $4.80!

We enjoyed all of these trips, but I was too young to enjoy them fully. For instance, after returning to Colorado Springs from Cripple Creek, a journey by narrow-gauge railroad through immensely scenic country, I remember telling Uncle Ben: "Well, another three dollars gone to the dogs!" That was the cost of the trip. It required more maturing on my part and additional trips to the state before I concluded that Colorado had more variety and beauty per square inch than any other state in the union. In 1914 I was super-patriotic and immensely loyal to my native state, Illinois, and thought no other could come close to it. If I saw something, like a piece of agricultural machinery or whatever, that was manufactured in Illinois, I felt like getting down and hugging it!

Soon after our return from Colorado Springs, father took other family members on the same tour. Father, Milt, Dorothy, Aunt Emma, Lydia (Grandma) Smith, and a Miss Anna Sweitzer from Pennsylvania who worked for us, constituted the group.

At the same time, Uncle Ben, Jacob Diller from Ontario, who worked a while for us on the sanitarium farm, and I took a trip to Denver to see the sights in that area. On the way home we stopped off briefly at Colorado Springs. I remember attending one session of a Billy Sunday revival meeting going on in the city at that time. Dad bought a copy of the song book used by Rodeheaver and Sunday in these meetings. The book has the following inscription in it: "J. J. Smith, Colorado Springs, June 1914."

I don't remember any part of the sermon, but I do remember something else Billy said. A lady in the audience had a crying baby with her and that irked Sunday. To my astonishment, as I recall the incident, he asked his ushers to take that heifer with that bawling calf outside. I would question my own memory of this occurrence, but Tim, who was not at the meeting, and I heard dad tell the story later. Billy was given to the use of strong and forceful language on occasion that was a bit unusual for a preacher. At another meeting dad told us how Sunday was irritated by a woman who left the meeting at a critical juncture during the sermon. Billy is supposed to have stated that there goes a daughter of the devil. The woman, having heard the remark, turned around and is alleged to have waved and said to Sunday, "Goodbye, Papa!" During World War I Sunday at times also used extreme language, especially about the Germans. But in fairness to the evangelist, I should say that I heard him speak several times at Winona Lake, Indiana, in the 1920s when I found his language in line with his helpful and biblical messages.

One thing that helped make my sojourn in Colorado more acceptable was the family automobile. Father had purchased a Buick just the previous December, and we took it along to Colorado. Just as I loved to drive teams in the field at an early age, I thrilled when I had opportunity to drive the car. Father was generous in permitting me to do so—almost too generous sometimes. On one occasion, while visiting the Edwin Ebersole family north of La Junta near Cheraw, I took the children out for a ride. When I spied a sugar beet dump along the roadside I decided, to the consternation of my passengers, to drive over it. Farmers hauled their beets to these wooden structures, drove up a fairly steep incline, and at the top dumped their loads into open railway cars on a siding. Driving the car up the incline, I stopped a moment at the top, and also about half way down on the other side to show that everything was under control. I completed the process without incident. But the more I thought about this later, the more I questioned the wisdom of this foolhardy venture. What if that dump at the top had not been securely locked? The whole bunch could have been dumped into that railroad car! I think the Ebersoles had their doubts about this venture before I did. But we have had many good laughs about it since.

The Ebersoles were not the only ones who had questions or anxiety about such a young fellow being allowed to drive a car. Allen Erb was another. Either in late spring or probably early fall of 1914 he had come to La Junta and the sanitarium for some purpose which I have forgotten. Father had asked me to go to La Junta to meet him. There was a light fresh snow on the ground—just enough to make it a bit slippery in coming up the sanitarium hill. The rear wheels spun before we reached the top. After backing down and getting a better start I made it to the top without further incident. Allen told me later how uneasy he was in that ride, especially in going up that hill!

One other venture at La Junta stands the test of time a little better than the beet-dump episode mentioned above. William Jennings Bryan, Secretary of State under Woodrow Wilson, gave an address in La Junta in October 1914 during the congressional campaign of that fall. Whether I did it with the connivance of the Swink school officials or not I do not know, but I played hookey from school that day, took the train from Swink to go to La Junta to hear Bryan, and returned by train. I even remember the main thrust of his talk: "Do you want to be governed by Wall Street or by Washington?" With all my later interest in Bryan, it is a bit ironic that this was the only time I ever heard him in person. Mrs. Bryan was also there, as was William Jennings Bryan, Jr. I had the pleasure of talking with Bryan, Jr. about this in 1963 when I visited him in his home in Laguna Beach, California. He was a friend of the president of the Holly Beet Sugar Company, which had a factory in Swink.

Late in December 1914 we returned to Illinois for a short visit. But for me it proved to be the end of this particular Colorado interlude. In January 1915 father and Milt returned to Colorado for another year. Tim, who had gone to Illinois in September 1914 to live with Uncle Ed Oyers and attend school there, also returned to Colorado at the end of the school year in the spring of 1915. I lived with Uncle Bens and finished my grade school work at the Schertz school in May 1915.

I came back to "good old Illinois," having left the West unaware of La Junta's and Colorado's historical significance. La Junta ("the junction") was located at an important junction on the Santa Fe Trail, and important old Fort Bent was nearby. Even Kit Carson Avenue in the city and some of his relatives living there did not arouse me like they did later. In 1914 we did everything we could to avoid the old ruts of the Trail (for fear the car center would hit the earth between the ruts) and in later years—especially in 1941 during our travel over the Trail from Missouri to Santa Fe—we did everything we could to find them.

Despite my undeveloped historical sense I do remember from 1914 a few glaring headlines in the *Denver Post* to which we subscribed. One episode had to do with the bloody industrial strife between the Colorado Fuel and Iron Company, controlled by John D. Rockefeller, Jr., and the United Mine Workers of America. The other was the outbreak of World War I early in August.

Because of my living in Colorado in 1914 and returning to Illinois at the end of the year, my last two years of grade school were a bit mixed up. For some cause or other I was transferred to the eighth grade in Colorado, and finished my seventh grade work in Illinois. This switching did not frustrate me too much, and I actually began to like school better than before. Among the good teachers I had was my last one, Agnes Robertson. Despite her encouragement, however, I did not plan to go to high school after finishing the eighth grade.

One incident stands out in my memory in connection with taking the examinations at the county court house in Eureka in May 1915. While writing I noticed that the people standing around in the room who were supposed to be monitoring the examination had their heads buried in newspapers reading and commenting on news of the day. Curious, after the examination I went over to Stump's drug store and bought a *Chicago*

Tribune—the first paper I remember purchasing—to find out what all the excitement was about. It was the story of the sinking of the Lusitania with its huge loss of life including Americans. So I finished my grade school years when the world was making tremendous changes, a transition which some have called the "end of innocence."

CHAPTER 3
Interlude 1915-1917

As stated, when I completed grade school in May 1915, I had not planned to go to high school. To do so was not usual at that time, especially among Mennonites, even though some of my cousins were exceptions to the rule. Since I thought I would be a farmer, I saw no need at that time for "higher education."

Somehow or other—just how I do not know—we worked out a deal with Chris Wagner that I would work for him on his farm the balance of 1915 after graduating from the eighth grade in May. This of course meant living with the Wagner family, which I was glad to do since our families were good friends, including Noah one of their sons who was just a bit older than I. Two more of my boy friends, Walter Wagner and Chris Schertz, lived close by. This made it convenient for us to have "get-togethers" in the evening after work or on Sundays and holidays.

Wagners lived across the road from the Roanoke Mennonite Church and thus close to Uncle Ben and Aunt Emma with whom my sister Dorothy was living. The Wagners were a happy family with five daughters (Frieda, Alvina, Rose, Pearl, and Celestia) and two sons (Noah and Ezra). They accepted and treated me as a son and brother. I did not pretend to be worth as much as a full-time hired hand and did not ask for full wages. I received something like $22.00 or $25.00 a month, plus my board and room, which at Wagners was no small item. Barbara (Mrs. Chris) and her daughters were excellent cooks and set a table groaning with tasty food. I remember especially the large amounts of luscious strawberries they served during the summer, and the frequency of serving pie throughout the year, sometimes for breakfast.

On Saturday evenings it was customary especially for the younger set to go to town for "business." Noah and I, and often Chris (Schertz) and Walter (Wagner) took the Cole Eight and carried out the custom. The "business" included the occasional purchase of necessities—clothing, toiletry or whatever—plus ice-cream sodas and some things not so necessary such as Camel cigarettes and/or Havana cigars. I have to confess that in 1915 I did use the weed a bit. Another part of our "business" was to keep our eyes open for eligible young girls who were not averse to accepting dates for an hour or two—at least long enough to walk around awhile and get ice-cream sodas.

One day—I think it was Memorial Day—Chris Wagner decided to take the day off and take Noah and me with him to Peoria to visit the Barnum and Bailey circus. The main parts of the show were delightful entertainment and educational, but a few of the side shows did little to prepare us for the Sunday school lesson which followed the next day!

At my request, on the way home from Peoria the Wagners went by way of Metamora to leave me off at Uncle Joe Smith's just east of the village. Frank King and Laura Smith were married that evening, and I apparently was one of the few cousins (cousin to both of them) who received an invitation. In any case Art was wondering whether I really had received an invitation! Because of the full day in Peoria I arrived late—in fact too late for the long wedding sermon of Bishop Andrew Schrock.

In threshing time Noah and I teamed up to constitute one hand as we helped thresh at the neighboring homes which made up the threshing ring. In addition to being a year or so older than my fourteen years, Noah was heavier and stronger than I. Only once or twice during very hot weather did I have trouble from heat exhaustion, toward which I had a tendency ever since suffering from a heatstroke earlier.

During cornhusking time in the fall, Noah could "out-shuck" me. If I remember correctly, he occasionally reached the coveted goal of husking 100 bushels a day. I don't think I ever reached it.

The year 1915 was also the year of an unusual revival series at the Roanoke Mennonite Church. Clayton F. Derstine, a young minister born and reared in eastern Pennsylvania, and serving as a city missionary in Altoona (Pennsylvania), was the evangelist. The series was something of a sensation. A fluent speaker with a voluminous voice, he caused something of a sensation in this staid, Amish Mennonite community—not only because of his voice but also because of his messages. He introduced Fundamentalism and dispensationalism with all its fine points about the end-times—or at least he gave these newer ideas a tremendous push. Later that same year Derstine accepted a call to serve as minister at Roanoke and thus became a powerful influence in the development of Fundamentalism not only in the local congregation but also throughout the Conference and Middle West.

The summer of 1915 passed quite rapidly, and after cornhusking my contract was to terminate. I looked forward to reuniting with the family when they returned from Colorado near the end of December. None in the family was a great letter writer, but I did receive a few communications from family members. Since Uncle Bens, with whom Dorothy was staying, lived closeby, I was often with them over weekends. Even so, Dot wrote me in July: "Dear Woody, Why don't you come home some evening so I can play with you [?] Your loving sister Dorothy." Milt and Tim wrote me once or twice from La Junta but I find no letters in my collection from dad. Tim wrote at least one letter under compulsion. Grace King who worked for dad and the family at La Junta in 1915 wrote me in September that she told Tilman "several times to write to you but he hadn't gotten it done. Now Mrs. Chris (Wagner) told him to and he did." Mrs. Wagner, for whom I was working, had been visiting her daughter Frieda in Colorado Springs and stopped in La Junta to visit our family. Grace also reported that Tim and Milt had been croqueting that evening, and then added: "It surely seems funny. Milton is as fat as ever."

Just as I had an unusual experience serving as a "hired hand" in 1915, I had another new experience the following winter. Uncle Ed Oyer and family went to Hesston, Kansas, where uncle could take in the winter Bible term, and asked Bill Schrock of Metamora and me to "operate" their farm while they were gone. Such "operation" in winter time was very simple—at least Bill and I made it so. We had an understanding that Bill would be responsible primarily for the chores outside and I would be responsible primarily for the housework. Since the housework included some "cooking" I'm afraid Bill got the worst of the deal! But he was a good, generous partner and took my limitations as a cook and housekeeper in stride. We "managed" to eat with relatives and other friends as often as possible, but we did eat sometimes at home. Potatoes and fried-down sausage, of which Aunt Ella had a good supply, were our staples. There were often leftovers, and occasionally the potatoes were "left over" so long that they got moldy. We had a lot of fun about this experience then and for years thereafter. Both of us survived and apparently were none the worse for the experience.

One episode turned out totally different than expected. Uncle Ed had said when we needed some cash to supply the family larder we should sell a load of oats.

Early in January I took a wagon load to sell at the grain elevator in Metamora. My brother Tim, who with the others had just returned from Colorado, went with me. Just after delivering the oats, while still in town, an automobile passed our wagon and scared our horses. They ran away, out of control, and failed to negotiate a turn in the road. During the process the team ran into a telephone pole, broke the wagon tongue, and then tore down the road with a stump tongue dragging on the ground. Soon this stump got caught in the ground. This threw the front end of the wagon upward, dumping both Tim and me. But Tim was fortunate enough to land in the wagon box uninjured. I was thrown clear of the wagon and landed on the crushed-rock road. The team broke loose from the wagon and ran home some three or four miles, to the great surprise and consternation of Bill Schrock. The driver of the car that scared our horses was Ben Schertz (cousin, not Uncle Ben), who took us immediately to Dr. Knoblauch whose office was nearby. My face was a bit bloody and I seemed to have double vision. But it soon cleared up. Ben took us to Uncle Sam Smith's where father and our new mother, who had gotten married in Pennsylvania the previous December 24th, were visiting for a few days. I then moved back with Bill and resumed my duties at Uncle Ed's until they returned from Kansas a month or so later.

Probably in February some time I was reunited with my family on the old farm which we had left two years before. I still had no intention of going further with my formal education. So I again settled down on the farm having no vocational plans for the future other than farming. I do remember how Tim, Milt, and I, together with Elmer King from Kansas who had come to work for us during 1916 and 1917, would jocularly talk about our vocational plans for the future. On one occasion in late spring father had put us to work in a cornfield replanting missing hills of corn that had been eaten by worms which thrived in cornfields that had been sod pasture in previous years. Engaging in kid talk along with our "hard" labor, we talked about what we wanted to do when we "grew up." Having recently read about the automobile racer, Barney Oldfield, who had accomplished the incredible feat of traveling a mile a minute, I added two options to farming. I said I wanted to be an automobile racer like Barney Oldfield or a preacher like Derstine, seeing no particular incongruity between the two.

A few minutes later this peaceful scene of "hard labor" in the cornfield suddenly changed. What brought on the heated discussion and disagreement I do not remember. But I vividly remember the fight that followed. Tim and Elmer were the villains in the piece, and Milt and I were the upholders of vitue and righteousness. Clods of sod were our missiles. I don't remember the outcome too well, but since for some time thereafter I had acquired a new nickname, "Derstine", I presume the side of virtue won.

More seriously, in 1917 and 1918 I did begin to rethink the matter of vocations, but that reassessment and final decision came slowly. In 1917 something happened which changed the course of my life. For some time Elmer King, our cousin and hired hand from Hesston, Kansas, kept telling me that I ought to go to school at Hesston, at least for one year, and see how I would like it. Furthermore, he added, you could also visit the King relatives at Hesston and Hutchinson. At first I paid little attention to what Elmer said. But as time went on, I began to think more about it, especially the point about visiting the King relatives. I am not sure but what this point about visiting the relatives was more of a determinant in my decision to go than getting a year of high school.

This decision did not come easily. I was enjoying life on the farm with its pleasures as well as its work. My old neighborhood cronies were still available—Ed Smith, Noah Wagner, Walter Wagner, Chris Schertz and others would join us boys in fun-making activities—going to the old swimming hole, engaging in Halloween pranks, attending a basketball game in Roanoke, or what have you. One basketball game in Roanoke stands out in memory, and I shall never forget it, especially what happened immediately afterward. We went to a restaurant for refreshments and I tied the horse I was riding to a post in front of the restaurant. While we were eating the electric lights went out. Imagine my consternation when shortly I discovered that my horse had gotten against a guy-wire which brought a transformer crashing to the street with live wires lying around! Fortunately and almost incredibly no one stepped on them even in the darkness. Ed Husseman, the one in charge of the electric utilities, soon turned off the power, and a major tragedy was, thank God, avoided.

Father not only permitted us to go to the basketball game, he paid the bill for the damages without complaint to or criticism of me. He was a good disciplinarian but reasonable and broadminded in administering it. For example, one time in my mid-teens I wanted to see what a movie was like, and, even though our home and church taught against attending the cinema, father gave me the money to attend one.

Another "social activity" we enjoyed in summer was going to the "ole swimming hole" a few miles southeast of us in Panther Creek near the Joseph Yordy home. Here the Yordy boys—especially Walter, Jonas, and Alvin—usually joined us. We swam in our "natural" swimming suits, barely knowing what the manufactured kind was like.

41

Mentioning the Yordy boys reminds me of another activity, quartet singing, which I started before going to Hesston and pursued further thereafter. Walter and Alvin Yordy sang tenor, Walter Zook second bass, and I baritone. Upon returning from Hesston during the summers we would resume our singing.

In addition to quartet singing, I became interested in taking private lessons in voice training. Either in 1916 or 1917 I took voice lessons from Professor Breeden at Eureka College. One of the first songs he had me purchase was "The Night has a Thousand Eyes." He was a good tenor singer and I think a good voice teacher. How many lessons I took I do not remember, but enough to get me interested. Professor Breeden also told me about a great singer who was coming to Peoria shortly and urged me to go hear her. She was Galli-Curci, one of the great singers of all time. I have heard many stars since then; but Galli-Curci stands out as one of the greatest. I was always grateful to Professor Breeden for introducing me to this new world.

One further episode which belongs to the pre-Hesston years must have occurred about 1916 or 1917. We had an automobile then (in fact two of them; dad had bought a Chevrolet in 1916), but the roads must have been bad, and so Tim and I went to Roanoke in the single-seated klondike to buy groceries. This was in the days when you could buy six loaves of bread for a quarter. On the way home I decided to smoke a cigarette. As stated before, I did a bit of this in 1915, but I was not accustomed to doing it after dad returned from Colorado in December. So I am not sure where I got the cigarette. I hardly would have bought a whole pack to get and smoke one cigarette. In any case the experience turned out to be an embarrassing one. I of course did not want father to know about this. So I opened the windows of the klondike to keep it well ventilated in order that there would be no smell of smoke to disclose the "classified" information. Imagine my petrification when after smoking some time the back window fell down and broke when it hit my head! Now what was going to happen to the "classified" information? My mind is blank as to what happened. But the problem must have been solved without serious confrontation with father. Otherwise I would remember the results more readily.

This was a period also when as a teenager of fifteen and sixteen I began to cast eyes on the opposite sex. In this respect I suppose I was normal, and so were the girls who turned their eyes in the direction of us boys. Again, father did not discourage me when I occasionally asked him for the car to have a date with this or that young girl.

These were pleasant, happy years, and they passed all too quickly. Almost before I knew it, September 1917 had arrived, the time I was to go to Hesston and secure a "higher education" even if it took a whole year!

CHAPTER 4
The Hesston Years 1917-1921

Due in no small part to Elmer King's influence I made my decision some time in the summer of 1917 to go to Hesston. Father's support also of course helped me to decide. Taking the local Santa Fe passenger train from Roanoke, I changed to the main line at Streator and arrived in Newton, Kansas, near Hesston, very early the next morning. Some one from the King family met me at Newton and helped me settle in at Green Gables which served as a dormitory and classroom building. Green Gables was a coed dormitory long before the current controversy on that subject arose! Classrooms and administrative offices were on the first floor, the girls on the second, and the boys on the third. The kitchen and dining room were in the basement. A new administration and classroom building was under construction but would not be ready for use fully until the fall of 1918.

I registered for the regular academy freshman courses: English under Paul Erb, Latin I under Alta (Mrs. Paul) Erb, Ancient History under Melvin Landis, Algebra under Mrs. Erb, Gospels under D. H. Bender, Music I and Chorus under C. K. Lehman. After studying these courses for ten days or two weeks, I decided to make one switch. Since I was planning to be there but one year and then return to farming in Illinois, I reasoned that Latin wasn't going to help me on the farm and that agriculture would be much more useful. So I made that change. J. B. Kanagy was the teacher.

This new venture proved an interesting, not to say exciting, one. The fairly frequent visits to uncle Sam Kings, two and a half miles southeast of Hesston, add-

45

ed much pleasure. Uncle Sam and Aunt Anna and of course the children enjoyed having company, relatives as well as others. They had so much company that Uncle Sam would complain to the guests how expensive it was to feed so many people, and would illustrate by pointing out the high cost of butter or any of the other items being passed at the table. With regard to butchering hogs he would say they butcher ten each year—two for themselves and eight for the college, meaning for the students who visited them. Guests unacquainted with him were shocked at first, but soon caught on and enjoyed his humor along with those who knew him. The visits to Hutchinson, equally enjoyable, were much less frequent because of distance.

Though I knew I would enjoy visiting the King relatives, I found my studies more interesting than anticipated and school life very enjoyable. Making acquaintances and friendships with people from various parts of the United States and Canada was a joy that has provided lasting satisfaction. Going to school in Kansas where there were many so-called Russian Mennonites was also a broadening experience. These were General Conference Mennonites, who operated Bethel College in Newton, Mennonite Brethren who operated Tabor College in Hillsboro, the Church of God in Christ, Mennonite, and a few smaller groups. Some of Hesston's students were from these bodies, especially the General Conference. The incongruity of having three Mennonite colleges within thirty miles of each other was not as apparent to me then as it was later. For, after all, to an (old) Mennonite in the late teens, GC Mennonites had strayed almost as far from true Christianity as the other "worldly" churches, such as Presbyterians and Methodists.

One of the highlights of that first year was to go to Lindsborg, Kansas, during the Easter season and listen to a rendition of Handel's "Messiah" by the Bethany College chorus. The Swedes at Lindsborg had developed a tradition of fine music, and their Messiah Festival during Passion Week had become world-famous. A large chorus—between 400 and 500—with orchestra and excellent soloists provided inspiring performances that left indelible impressions on me. During each Passion Week for the next three years I was drawn back to Lindsborg to hear the "Messiah". In a way, these performances spoiled me. To this day I don't care to hear the "Messiah" unless it is given well. I say this in spite of the fact that we gave the "Messiah" at Hesston while I was there, and I shared with Melvin Landis the singing of the bass solos, and we sang it without any musical accompaniment!

The first year passed all too rapidly. I enjoyed my courses and the extra-curricular activities. By the spring of 1918 I began to reassess my plans, especially my earlier decision to spend only one year at Hesston. I wrote to dad asking him if I could come back to Hesston two more years, adding that I believed I could finish the academy in that time. Again he was cooperative and gave his permission.

These were eventful and significant years. There was of course further broadening of my horizon. Included in my registration in September 1918 was Latin I which I had dropped the year before. In fact I took three years of it at Hesston, and have never regretted it. It probably helped my English almost as much as the English courses I took. Other language courses I took at Hesston—German I under Gustav Enss and New Testament Greek under Harold S. Bender—were less fruitful, the reason being I took only one year of each.

It is not necessary to mention all of the courses taken, but some stand out in memory, if not significance, more than others. One of these was "The Christian

Fundamentals'' taught by President D. H. Bender. I still have the textbook we used, *The Great Doctrines of the Bible*, by William Evans of Moody Bible Institute. The book portrays the Fundamentalist, premillennial view. Bender accepted the author's view pretty largely. But I do recall that in discussing Matthew 25 Bender stated he had difficulty in getting away from the old (amillennial) idea that there will be one general judgment and one resurrection instead of two with a 1000 years in between.

Be that as it may, I came out of Hesston a strong, premillennialist Fundamentalist. Among others, J. B. Smith, who had left Hesston shortly before I arrived, influenced the institution in this direction. Gustav Enss also was a strong Fundamentalist. The Scofield Bible, which Hesston promoted and through its bookstore sold in large numbers to us students, also had its effect. One of the most foolish things I ever did—either in my academy senior or college freshmen year—was to consent in a weak moment to teach an extra-curricular Bible class that someone else, better prepared, was supposed to teach and could not. We used Larkin's text with its detailed charts of the end-time. One of the students in the class, Dan Driver, was apparently not too impressed with the quality of the text or of the teaching! And I could not blame him! Dan had a way of asking pesky questions. When discussing the details of Christ's second coming—the first and second resurrections with the 1000 years in between, the rapture, the great tribulation, et cetera—Dan would ask, "How do you know it's going to happen just like that?" In a response that was supposed to satisfy all reasonable inquiring minds, the teacher oracularly proclaimed: "Right here it is on the chart!" But Dan's mind was not satisfied. Nor in fact was my own!

We Hesston students also had good-natured fun trying to enlighten Bethel College students and faculty on Bible doctrines. A few of the faculty—for example, Samuel Burkhard and O. B. Gerig—were graduates of Goshen College, which, in view of their "heretical" ideas, made Goshen as well as Bethel suspect in our young, tender minds.

My missionary zeal extended also to Harold S. Bender, one of my teachers at Hesston and later at Goshen. Harold was pretty "sound," but there was one place where I thought he could improve. He was an amillennialist instead of a premillennialist. Having become quite a theological authority by virtue of my graduation from Hesston Academy, and having had D. H. Bender's courses on the Gospels and Bible doctrines, plus Old Testament and New Testament history, I felt I should confront my good friend Harold with the clear, biblical teaching on the subject, especially Revelation 20. This occurred during a visit in his home in Elkhart, Indiana, in June 1920. Tim and I were enroute from Hesston to Michigan, to which our family had moved in January. But Harold was not impressed with my lucid biblical argument, and I failed in my attempt to get him to see the clear light of biblical truth! But maybe it was just as good for the Mennonite theological world that I didn't succeed in converting him. In any case, I have had many good laughs since then when thinking about my brash, juvenile efforts.

The options in music, in which I was also interested, were quite limited at Hesston. As I recall, Music I and Music II, and voice lessons under Arthur Slagel composed the courses offered. The school had no pianos at that time, which meant, of course, that there was no piano instruction, nor were they used for accompanying vocal music.

While singing oratorios like Sullivan's "Light of the World" and Handel's "Messiah" without a good instrumental accompaniment left much to be desired, the quality of much of Hesston's vocal presentations was remarkably high. The school had a number of outstanding singers. For example, I remember how thrilled I was when I heard Siddie Oyer, Ida White, Martin Weaver, Paul Erb, Melvin Landis, and another whose name has escaped me, sing the "Sextet From Lucia." The performance would have been a creditable one in larger concert halls.

Other musical groups, especially quartets, were also popular on the campus. The first year I was there, C. L. Graber from Wayland, Iowa, Edward Yoder from Kalona, Iowa, Stanley Brubaker from near Kitchener, Ontario, and I formed a group called the Apollo Quartet.

We practiced and sang for the fun of it, but we were frequently called on to sing at various kinds of programs. After the first year we had to reorganize, and I do not recall the other members, except Martin Weaver with whom I sang some. The last year or two I was there I remember forming the "Nightingale Quartet," composed of Walter Schertz from near Metamora, Illinois, Tillman Erb (Jr.) from Hesston, Walton Clemmer from Eastern Pennsylvania, and myself.

One curious, brief episode grew out of my acquaintance with Walton Clemmer. He was not only an excellent bass singer, but also an able salesman. He told me how much he was making by working part-time selling magazines—so much so in fact that he inveigled me into trying my hand at it. I had visions of how much money I could make in such promisingly fertile territory as nearby Hutchinson and Wichita. But I thought I would be modest about it and learn the tricks of the trade in smaller Newton. So one Saturday morning I took "Old Jerkey" (the train) to Newton and started down the street nearest the station. At the door of the first house where I stopped, the lady said they were not interested. I think I was selling—rather trying to sell—the American Magazine, among others. At the second house the reply was the same. The third and fourth efforts were equally "successful." Some were courteous and some slammed the door on me. But all the "transactions" were equally "profitable." I soon lost patience and gave up the effort, exclaiming, "Thank God, I don't have to do this to make a living!" I charged the morning's experience to education and learned quickly—possibly too quickly—that I was not a salesman.

During these happy, serene years at Hesston, tumultuous events were occurring in the outside world which sooner or later were bound to affect our sheltered lives. When World War I broke out in July 1914 few Americans thought their country would become directly involved as it finally did in April 1917. The draft which Congress and the Wilson administration put into effect missed me by a month but caught many other male students.

Among other dislocations, the war likely made worse and helped spread the serious influenza epidemic in the fall of 1918. So many of us students became ill, along with family members at home, that school was closed for three weeks. Either before or after I had a bout with the disease I—accompanied by Sam King—went home to help husk corn. I shall never forget the return trip to Hesston. Even before starting on November 10 there were false rumors about the armistice having been signed. Some of these reports were put over our party telephone line, only to be superseded a little later by another message that the first report was false. Finally,

51

after midnight on the morning of November 11, Walter Schertz, another Illinois student, and I—Sam had to go earlier because of the draft—began to hear some of the most ungodly noises as we passed through the cities of eastern Kansas. It was some time before we discovered what the noise was all about: celebrating the signing of the armistice. Nor shall I ever forget what I saw later that morning in the supposedly peaceful, staid city of Newton. Part of the celebration here consisted of dragging behind trucks stuffed-rag dummies representing the German Kaiser, with men sitting on the back end of the vehicles pumping bullets into the Kaiser!

Soon however such passionate outbursts subsided, and all were happy that the war was over. The broadening of my horizons, mentioned earlier, included further thinking on my vocational goals, which now included other possible options in addition to farming. Hesston had a Christian Worker's Band for those who were not yet certain what work they should take up but who wanted to follow the Spirit's leading in the matter. That made sense to me and I joined it. Missionary work and teaching were also looming up as possibilites.

New social relationships were also in the making. I had dated some fine girls in Illinois, and I did the same at Hesston. I had pleasant relationships with all of them. Among others, I began to date in my sophomore year Verna Graber who came from Wayland, Iowa. She was a sister of C. L. Graber with whom I had sung in a quartet, and of Joseph D. Graber who was to become one of my closest friends and buddies in the years to come. More—much more—will be said later about the relationship with Verna. She became the most important pilgrim I met on the trail and has traveled with me since.

In 1919 Tim also joined me at Hesston. He had remained out of school three years to help on the farm, in contrast to my two. Milt joined me in 1921 and was with me only a few months since I had to leave the last of October because of health reasons.

In my senior year my class honored me by electing me president. This meant some additional extra-curricular activities, which included preparing an address on the class motto, "Not Evening But Dawn." I took my assignment seriously and put in much time in preparing the speech. In order that their president might give an address of which they did not need to be ashamed, some class members—I remember especially Emma Harnish—helped me with the speech. As I look back from the eighties and reread the oration I have to smile at the "noble effort." It contains the usual platitudes found in high school students' commencement speeches: We face "life with all its problems and perplexities. We are at the threshold of an unknown future." And then I added this clarifying profundity: "Indeed we know not what the future has in store for us." Also I am afraid I was not as careful as I should have been about the use of quotation marks. But I was serious and sincere about it, and after more than sixty years I still stand by the central thrust of the address: if we live in the center of God's will no life will be cut off in incompleteness, no matter whether it is called home in the morning, at noon-tide, or in the evening of life.

After graduation that spring Tim and I had a new home to which to go. In January 1920, our family which now included George born in February 1917, moved to a farm between St. Johns and Ashley, Michigan. Father sold the farm at the unheard-of price of $500 per acre, and bought what he thought was equally good land in Michigan for $140 per acre. He, mother, George and Milt went up in the Ford in

January of 1920, and Tim and I drove up the old Cadillac early in June. I wasn't home very long until Alvin King from Hesston dropped by on his way to Flint to purchase a new Buick for his agency. (Later he became well known for selling Fords.) Alvin asked me to ride along with him to Chicago and then return by train. That way we could have a good visit together and could also visit our cousin Emma Oyer who was a worker at the Mennonite Home Mission. This appealed to me, and dad gave me permission. I had a good visit with Alvin, and also with Emma. But I had more. Emma, who often attended meetings at Moody Bible Institute, said I came at the right time. They were having special meetings (Founder's Week) at Moody's which she urged me to attend along with her. I was very happy to go.

I discovered that not only was Moody's celebrating Founder's Week, the World Conference on Christian Fundamentals was having its second annual session there at the same time. Since I, as an upholder of the orthodox view of Christianity and the Bible, had become, as stated above, quite Fundamentalistic in my orientation, I was delighted with this opportunity. I attended not only that one day but came back for one or two more. Unfortunately I don't remember which speakers I heard, except H. A. Ironside. James M. Gray, William B. Riley, R. A. Torrey, J. C. Massee, John R. Straton, and A. C. Dixon were some of the Fundamentalist leaders in those years. My interest in the Fundamentalist Movement is evidenced by the fact that I purchased at this conference a report of the first World Conference on Fundamentals, held at Philadelphia the year before, in May 1919. Entitled *God Hath Spoken*, the book contains the twenty-five addresses delivered at the 1919 conference, together with an introduction and the reports of various committees.

So this book has become a historic one. This trip to Chicago—the chance decision for which was made in a light-hearted moment for the purpose of visiting cousin Alvin enroute—turned out to be much more significant than anticipated.

After working for father on the farm at Ashley during the summer I returned to Hesston in September as a college freshman. In the spring of 1920 I had agreed with the college administration to serve as hall manager for men, nearly all of whom, except the local residents, lived in Green Gables. Financially, this made it easier for me to return. By this time I had decided to finish college. Titus Lapp of Roseland, Nebraska, was assistant hall manager. The work of hall manager involved maintaining order in the dormitory, seeing to it that the rules were carried out, and taking the roll in chapel, attendance at which was required. The rules were quite strict, with at least one of which I was not in sympathy. Chewing gum on the campus was prohibited. But this did not cause any great problem while I was hall manager, even though the cleaning force would find fairly large amounts of chewing gum wads stuck on the bottom of chairs, desks, and elsewhere. One time while walking on the campus with student Levi Miller, President Bender ran across a cigar butt. He asked: "Levi, did you leave this here?" In his drawling manner which only those who knew him can appreciate, Levi replied: "I don't know. But it must have come from the faculty because the students aren't allowed to smoke."

On the whole, my experiences as hall manager were pleasant ones. I was not satisfied, however, with the way the administration handled one disciplinary case. Several students were disciplined for infraction of the rules, including smoking, and one was sent home. I objected because I was not assured the one sent home had the same equal hearing, before the decision was made, that the others had had.

Though a busy year, I took time to enter the college oratorical contest. Having heard and read much about the suffering caused by the war, I chose the subject "The Cry of the Children." As I read it now, I see it was something of a tear-jerker. The result of the contest was a strange one, and I have never been quite able to figure it out to this day. I placed first in content, Harry Brunk got first in delivery, and Guy F. Hershberger somehow slipped in ahead of both of us and won the contest!

By this time I was thinking of a college major and had in mind history and music as possible options. Since Hesston was very weak in music, and Bethany at Lindsborg was very strong in that field I decided to transfer there in September of 1921. I registered for various courses, including American history as well as voice and piano. I got a good rooming place in the home of Professor Pihlblad, son of the college president, with a ministerial student by the name of Johnson as roommate.

Things went well for a brief period, and I started practicing with the famous chorus that was to render the "Messiah" the following Easter season. Soon however I developed sinus trouble and a cold that I had trouble shaking off. After about two weeks I went to Hesston to consult with friends, and we decided I had better return to Hesston. The administration there gave me a course to teach—Music I—which helped me financially. I regretted having to leave Bethany, but I appreciated Hesston's fine cooperation.

Here too things seemed to go well for a time, but the cold I had did not leave me. To make a long story short, at the end of October Dr. Wedel of Hesston diagnosed my case as tuberculosis. This of course required a drastic change in my well-laid plans, and I decided to go to the Mennonite Sanitarium at La Junta, Colorado, to recuperate. Hesston arranged a farewell service for me in which our Nightingale Quartet participated. I also gave my personal testimony in singing a solo which has meant a great deal to me since. The song, "I Cannot Always Trace the Way," has a simple tune but a profound message:

I cannot always trace the way
Where Thou, Almighty One, dost move;
But I can always, always say
That God is love.

When mystery clouds my darkened path,
I'll check my dread, my doubts reprove;
In this my soul sweet comfort hath,
That God is love.

Yes, God is love, a word like this,
Can evr'y gloomy tho't remove;
And turn all tears, all woes to bliss,
For God is love.

Though living among friends, the simple, profound message of that song was what I needed when I received that news about my health two weeks after I had turned twenty-one.

CHAPTER 5
Detour 1921-1926

Using the word detour reminds me of the not-well-traveled American who years ago visited Canada. When he returned he was asked how the roads were up there. He replied that they had two kinds. Those that were built by the Englishman, Mr. King (Kings Highways) were pretty good. But those built by the Frenchman, Mr. Detour, were terrible.

There were factors in my "detour" that made the traveling pretty rough, particularly for the first year or two. But there were other factors that made it—when all over and looked back upon—a tremendous experience. Going to La Junta was a natural for me. It was our church institution, I had lived there in 1914, and knew quite a few people there, including some of the nurses and doctors and Allen Erb the superintendent. Allen met me at the train, took me to the sanitarium about five miles west of La Junta, and his sister Ruth Erb, whom I had known at Hesston, says she admitted me. I soon became acquainted with others of the staff and found them a capable group dedicated to the work of restoring wholeness to life, physically and spiritually.

The kind words which came my way from many, many friends at Hesston on the occasion of my leaving constitute a treasury of precious memories from which I have frequently drawn and which I can never forget. These too have helped make "the rough places plain." One businessman in Hesston—J. C. Swartz—who was unable to attend the farewell service at the college, wrote me a letter that same evening to express his sorrow and best wishes. He mentioned some things that I had done for him and his family that I had forgotten.

"To you it may seem strange," he wrote, "that I have a sadness at heart that you are leaving. My only prayer for you is that God may speedily restore you to perfect health so you may go on doing good all your days. You will never know the disappointment I feel right now that I did not get to be at your farewell meeting." Receiving a letter with such contents, and more, was a humbling experience. I could only pray that through the grace and power of God I would not let my friends down.

This support from family and friends continued through my illness and was a tremendous factor in winning the battle for health. In this regard no one was more important than my girl friend who later became my dear life companion. By the time I left Hesston for La Junta in the fall of 1921 Verna and I had dated considerably and had begun to develop a serious relationship which made us feel more and more that we wanted to travel the trail together. We did not become engaged formally until June 1923 when I visited her in her home in Noble, Iowa. But the decision was made in fact—if not in so many words—in July 1922 by correspondence.

Not making as rapid progress as I thought I ought, in June or July I asked Dr. Kerley, the doctor who I thought knew most about my case, to tell me frankly what he thought my chances for recovery were. He replied about fifty-fifty. Thinking about this not so optimistic prognosis, I felt I ought to be honest with Verna and report it to her; and since my future was thus uncertain, I thought I ought to offer to release her of any obligation to continue the relationship. My letter even unnerved her a bit that I should ever have thought that she would want to stop the relationship because of my illness. She would be glad to stop, she emphasized over and over, if it would be to the best interests of my health, or if for any reason *I* really wanted to discontinue. But if it was for her sake, then I should forget it. What was a friend for, she wrote, if she could not stand by me when she was needed? This and the following letter were the most beautiful and precious I have ever received. Really they were what I had expected. But I have been amazed ever since at the love, loyalty and devotion which the writer of the letters portrayed. And they are symbolic of a lifetime together.

Life at La Junta was not very active physically. This was a time when they were emphasizing the "rest-cure." Although I had bathroom privileges, I was supposed to be in bed for a certain period—I have forgotten whether it was six weeks or three months. I of course was subjected to many tests, X-ray and others. Dr. Stickles had various ideas he wanted to try out on me, and I had the feeling at times that I was a sort of experimental guinea pig. But I did not feel that the time in bed was wasted. We mad-rushing Americans are always too much in a hurry and never give life time to catch up with us. So when one is in bed for several months one has time to contemplate what life is all about and sort out the trivial from the important. I remember telling Paul Erb who visited me at La Junta that I thought this would be a better world if everyone had to spend a few months in bed.

Time had a way of passing on even at La Junta. Letters had to be answered, friends came to visit, programs and entertainment were provided. A Victrola provided good music for the musically inclined. I played over and over Lucille Marsh's rendition of "Come Unto Me" and "I Know That My Redeemer Liveth," and Elsie Baker's recording of "One Sweetly Solemn Thought." Maurice T. Brackbill, college student at Hesston and later professor at Eastern Mennonite College (EMC), gave—his first performance I

61

believe—his inspiring lecture "The Glory of the Sunset." Another high point was the program that the touring Bluffton College Men's Glee Club gave in the summer of 1922. Boyd Smucker, good friend of my uncle C. Henry Smith, and who with Smith moved from Goshen College to Bluffton in 1913, gave as part of the program his reading "Over the Hill to the Poorhouse." He and others were quite surprised to learn that I was C. Henry's nephew.

The patients were of a motley assortment. As I recall, the Mennonites were in a minority. In fact at the moment I cannot remember many Mennonite names. But I do recall some. One of these was Martha Swartzendruber, Minnie's sister. We had many good conversations together. We were kindred spirits, and we discussed everything from bonnets, capes and plain coats to—whatever. Both of us had come by way of Hesston, and both of us were mavericks on subjects such as the above.

One patient came under unusual cirumstances. I think it was in 1922 and the ultimate consequences were also unusual. It is the story of Maude Buckingham and her husband. Allen Erb gives the story in some detail in his *Privileged to Serve* (65-67). Suffice it to say here, Maude was taking her very sick husband from Arkansas to Colorado Springs in search of his health. A La Junta resident found them along the roadside west of the city, the man exhausted and lying on the ground. The La Junta resident decided to bring the couple to the sanitarium. Erb took him in and ministered to his needs. The wife said she would work to pay her husband's expenses. He was so ill, however, that the administration decided to remove him to the La Junta City Hospital which the Mennonites were also now operating. In a way, the story has a sad ending. After some time the husband died. But in a more significant way, the story has an ending in which victory, rejoicing and brightness clearly outshone the darkness. Mr. Buckingham became a Christian and requested baptism from Brother Erb. He left this world with a ringing testimony of victory and salvation. Maude too became a Mennonite Christian, decided to become a nurse, and go back to serve her people in Arkansas. This required much effort: paying for her husband's bills, finishing academy at Hesston, taking nurses training at La Junta, and doing it all on her resources.

In a larger more significant sense the story is still not ended; it continues to this day. For Maude later went back to Arkansas, and, with the blessing of the Mennonite district conference and the Mennonite Board of Missions, started Sunday schools, churches, and nursing clinics. The Mountain View (now Buffalo), Three Brothers, Mt. Joy, Culp, and Calico Rock churches, and the Calico Rock Medical Clinic are monuments today which resulted from ''helping a sick man and his wife when they needed help'' (Erb, 67) on a dusty road near La Junta, Colorado, in 1922!

In October 1922 I decided it was time for a change of scenery and went to Colorado Springs for a few weeks. I stayed with Mrs. Hough in Manitou. She had formerly lived in my community in Illinois. One main reason for going, in addition to wanting a change of scenery, was to see some specialists in pulmonary diseases. The trip was good for me. The doctors, noting good improvement in the short time I was there, gave me an encouraging report.

In December 1922 my correspondence included an unusual item from friends in Illinois. It was in the form of a Memorandum Book with messages from some thirty-five friends, the messages to be opened and read on different days. Some were short, others were longer.

They were all meaningful, coming as they did from old friends who wished to express their thoughtful concern in this way. The Chris Wagner family, for whom I had worked in 1915, engineered the project. Fortunately, I still have this memo book, and I treasure it highly.

Another highlight in December 1922 was a visit from my brother Tim. This was all the more meaningful to me because none of the other members of my immediate family was able to visit me at La Junta. Tim, a senior in the academy at Hesston, spent part of his Christmas vacation with me. He of course could make interesting comparisons with the time when he lived on the sanitarium farm in 1914 and 1915.

When I made the decision I do not remember, but by the spring of 1923 I had decided to go to Illinois. Dr. Smith of Eureka had a new medicine he was using with good success and thought he could help me. Uncle Ben and Aunt Emma wanted me to stay with them. Generous uncle and aunt! They have done more than their share of taking care of relatives and others!

Enroute I stopped off at Hesston to take in commencement and visit relatives. Tim was graduating with the academy class of 1923, and cousin Sam King with the college class of that year. In addition to the King relatives, I also visited Uncle C. Henry and Aunt Laura Smith. They were living in Newton that year while uncle was teaching at Bethel College and gathering material for his book, *The Coming of the Russian Mennonites: An Episode in the Settling of the Last Frontier*.

Also enroute to Eureka I had a good visit with Verna and her family at Noble, Iowa. In view of all the circumstances involved, this was a long-anticipated and most meaningful visit—how long I do not remember. Verna had graduated from Hesston academy in 1922 and had spent the past year teaching in a local elementary school. So she was now a veteran. We visited the old haunts, especially scenic Fern Cliff about two miles from Verna's home. Here was the ideal spot to become formally engaged, and we took advantage of the situation. But, as stated earlier, we had in practice and fact become engaged in July 1922 when Verna replied to my offer—because of the uncertain health prognosis—to release her from any responsibility to continue the relationship. So the past was prologue.

Once at Eureka, I immediately made contact with Dr. Smith and started treatments, which, as I recall, I took weekly for at least a few months. It may be that I took them less frequently in the months that followed. To my amazement I started gaining weight and went up from about 150 in the summer of 1923 to 200 by the spring of 1924. Of course Aunt Emma's good cooking was also an important factor. My improvement in Illinois seemed more marked and rapid than in Colorado. Of course I continued to rest a great deal also. And no doubt this improvement was predicated at least in part on the groundwork laid in Colorado. My association with my sister Dorothy, who continued to live with Uncle Bens, also made the year still more pleasant.

I of course also visited my family in Michigan as soon as possible. With the move to Michigan in 1920 where good land was much cheaper father thought he could improve himself economically. Due to several circumstances, however, this did not occur. Father had bought too much land, got himself spread out too much, and thus was not prepared for the depression which came in 1921 and hit agriculture especially hard. Land prices plummeted and remained low throughout the decade. A few dishonest people took advantage of his honest, trusting disposition, although this was a minor factor in causing his economic difficulties.

Unfortunately father's health began to fail in 1923

and got worse in 1924. I made several trips between Illinois and Michigan during the course of the year, and when he got worse in the spring of 1924 I went up to remain. Despite his serious illness (tuberculosis) we had good visits, and he left a ringing testimony of joy and victory through Christ. He passed on May 16, 1924. Services were held at the local Bethel Mennonite Church May 18 with Pastor George H. Summer in charge, assisted by Peter Ropp of Imlay City. Ezra Yordy and Henry R. Schertz officiated at the services at the Roanoke Mennonite Church in Illinois May 20. I was impressed by one of the songs, led by Walter E. Yoder, used at the service, "How Firm a Foundation." I was not used to hearing it at funerals, but the more I thought about it the more I thought, "How appropriate!" Father was buried in the cemetery nearby where mother was laid to rest in 1914.

Since father and mother had asked me to be administrator of the estate, I returned to Michigan soon after the funeral and after a trip to Iowa to visit Verna. Grandpa (C.S.) Schertz went along to Iowa to visit old friends, and we drove out in his Ford roadster. Some of us did a bit of joking about the trip. I said we went out to hold evangelistic meetings at Wayland, Grandpa serving as the evangelist and I as the song leader. We had to concede that we did not have many converts—only one, Verna. So we emphasized quality rather than quantity in this evangelistic tour!

In Michigan we were fortunate that both Tim and Milt could continue to help run the farm. We were fortunate also in being able to hire good men as farm laborers. This was important because both of my brothers wanted to complete their college studies as soon as possible. Milt left for Goshen College in September 1924 and Tim went one year later. They returned however during summer vacations to help on the farm. My own contribution to the physical labor of farm operations was still limited, and so my work was confined to management, business and the lighter tasks. I even took two years of Spanish by correspondence during this period. I made good grades, but this certainly is not the way to study a foreign language. At least it was not then, when I had no audio aids to give me practice in listening.

Since none of us three older boys wanted to farm, and George was too young, we decided to have a sale, rent the farms and eventually get rid of them. Mother too thought this was the best thing to do, and she decided to resume her old profession, nursing. She was very fortunate in having this professional skill to fall back on in case of necessity. From her Colorado days, where she had graduated from the Minnequa Hospital Nursing School in Pueblo, she was known as an excellent nurse and had no difficulty in getting and holding a job. After our sale fairly early in 1926, mother started nursing in the St. Johns Hospital and remained there until she retired in the 1960s.

I too wanted to finish my college studies and had no difficulty in deciding where to go. Since I had great respect for Sanford C. Yoder, the president of Goshen College, Noah Oyer the dean, C. L. Graber the business manager, and since Tim, Milt, Dot, and Verna were already there, the decision was made for me. At Goshen I stayed for some months with Uncle Bens who had moved from Eureka in 1924 so that Dot could enroll in the academy. George remained in Michigan to complete grade school and then joined us in Goshen to attend high school and college. So Goshen has been very important in the life of our family.

CHAPTER 6
Completing College:
Goshen 1926-1928

Lodging at Uncle Bens, I enrolled in summer school at Goshen in June 1926. I hoped to finish college in two years—with summer school—and Dean Noah Oyer helped me work out a tight schedule which met all the requirements but left very little room for electives. I had decided to major in history, minor in English, and meet requirements for a teacher's license in secondary schools. I took both semesters of United States history simultaneously under Guy F. Hershberger and a course in Field Zoology (really ecology) under S. W. Witmer. In this course we made numerous field trips to surrounding areas to study plants in their natural habitats. There were some six or seven students in the class—too many for all of us to pile into Witmer's Ford roadster. So four or five went in the car and two of us came along on bicycles behind pulled by ropes extended to us from the Ford—not the safest method of transportation in the world even in 1926 with fewer automobiles! For the U.S. history I chose the ambitious subject of the "History and Development of the Monroe Doctrine" for my term paper. I made A's in all three courses and felt good about my introduction to Goshen College.

In September 1926 I rented a room in the home of Harry Hartzlers, only a few doors from the campus on South Eighth Street. I took my meals in the college dormitory. This arrangement worked out very well, and I remained there until I graduated in June 1928.

These were delightful years. I enjoyed all of my courses, particularly, of course, those in my major field, history. Many of those in the administration and on the faculty, as well as some of the students, I had known at Hesston. The student body was small enough to be a close-knit family. Having two brothers and a sister here also enhanced the family characteristics of the student body. It is an interesting coincidence that our educational plans worked out in such a way that all three of us brothers—Tim, Milt and I—should have graduated in the same class. Since I was the oldest, my brothers had fun explaining to others that I was the most retarded! But since I was the only one in the family to secure a Ph.D.—they had M.A.s—they did not care to push the explanation too far.

In addition to my history courses under Guy F. Hershberger and Harold S. Bender, I took two economics courses under Ernst Correll who had recently come from Germany. Correll was quite a character. He was a jovial German who knew his economics better than the disciplinary art. Occasionally a few of his students took advantage of his good nature, and his classroom—even though composed of *college* students—was in danger of becoming a circus. One of his disciplinary methods was to throw a piece of chalk or an eraser at the offending student. The following is taken from the 1928 *Maple Leaf*: " 'Doc' Correll shouting at Milton Smith during Economics class: 'Say, Mr. Smith! Why can't you pay attention to what is being said? If you want to carry on a conversation with Miss Cook, why don't you get a date with her?' " Fat [Milt's nickname in those days] replied: 'I'm game! I'll go if you'll ask her.' " But we had fun and learned some economics. I also audited H. S. Bender's course in principles of sociology and Gustav Enss's in philosophy.

Professor John Umble, who was head of the English and Speech department for many years, and Ira Franck who was at Goshen a short time, were my English teachers. Paul Erb, visiting professor from Hesston in the summer of 1927 and later professor at Goshen, taught one of my semesters in American Literature.

I took most of my psychology and education courses under a Professor Hohn who taught at Goshen while Silas Hertzler was at Yale University completing his Ph.D. degree. Hertzler returned to Goshen midway through the summer session in 1927 and took over Hohn's courses. I am quite certain that this change resulted in getting at least two less A's than I would have received had Hohn continued. Hohn had been giving me A's, but Hertzler was down on that idea. Hertzler did break down, however, and gave me one A. In fact he had acquired the nickname, "Professor C-." On one occasion a student complained to Hertzler about getting a C- in one course. The complaint did not do any good, however, except that Hertzler did concede that the grade was "a strong C-." Even though known as a stiff grader, students respected him highly as a scholar and a man of integrity and helpfulness.

Especially in my senior year I was occupied a great deal with extra-curricular activities. In those days the YMCA and YWCA, which together constituted the YPCA (Young Peoples Christian Association), were important organizations—probably the most important on the campus. I was president of the YMCA, and coincidently, Verna was president of the YWCA. The YP was an umbrella organization under which most of the student organizations operated. Specifically each Y had the following committees, the work of which was indicated by the name: Devotional, Bible Study, Mission Study, Finance, Membership, Extension, Social, and Employment. The chairpersons of these committees made up the cabinet in each Y and met with its president to advise and discuss the organization's work. Just to mention one example of the significance of the Y's work, several of the Mennonite churches in the Goshen area originated as a result of its Extension Committee's activity.

I served also as vice president of the Mennonite Historical Society, and in my junior year as president of the Student Council—continuing as a member the following year—and president of the Men's Dormitory Association.

In April I was delighted to participate in one activity which was started by Uncle C. Henry Smith and N. E. Byers in the early days of Goshen College, the annual peace oratorical contest. B. F. Deahl, a local lawyer, provided the modest prize money. I spoke on "Must We Have War," and made a strong plea for the settlement of international disputes through courts of justice just as we handle domestic disputes. Sam Yoder got first prize, I got second, and Forrest Kanagy placed third. I was fortunate in winning anything, for the week before the contest I was in bed with the "flu" and was barely able to get out and participate on the day of the contest.

As to the central thrust of my oration, the years have not changed my view. I still believe that educated people—say nothing of Christian people—must come to the place where disputes will be settled peaceably by international courts of justice and arbitration rather than by might or force, which is what war means. We ought to be able to do this if we can conquer space and put people on the moon as we have. It would be a big help toward this end if we could change our priorities and spend at least part of the billions for peace that we now spend for war, defense, and conquering space.

Occasionally Americans see the vision in the distance but don't quite catch up with it, or at least soon lose it. Such was the case in the 1920s when we graduated from college. We had but recently fought "the war to end all wars," and Woodrow Wilson and others had launched the League of Nations to settle international disputes in the future. But Germany (and her allies) were not in it, and we compelled her to sign a peace (?) treaty which was characterized by one American diplomatic historian as the "peace which passeth all understanding." Yet the vision had not totally disappeared by 1928 when fifteen nations (more later) signed the Briand-Kellogg Pact outlawing war. Article I provided that the parties renounce war as an instrument of national policy, and Article II provided that disputes between the parties should never be settled except by pacific means. Unfortunately there were some interpretations added by the United States which weakened the declaration, especially the one that said the treaty did not outlaw wars of self-defense. But the people didn't bother about reading the fine print, and so the illusions of the 1920s continued.

The so-called Coolidge prosperity also added to the illusions of the decade. Calvin Coolidge, who as vice-president became president upon the death of Harding in 1923, had little to do with the prosperity—one writer says " he rode along with the procession with his face toward the rear"—but he and the Republican party got the credit for it. That made the Republican candidate in 1928, Herbert Hoover, a shoo-in in the battle against Alfred E. Smith. I remember giving a talk in speech class in the spring of 1928 on the topic "Why Al Smith Cannot Become President of the United States." I had four reasons: 1. He was Roman Catholic; 2. He was wet; 3. He was too much a part of Tammany Hall; 4. Economic prosperity. A political revolution occurred in our country in the years following so that reasons 1 and 2 were no longer important obstacles to success, but I think they still had some significance in 1928.

In the winter and spring of 1928, like most college seniors, I began looking for a job. I had prepared for high school teaching, and so I began looking for a position of teaching history. My preparation included a major in English, but I preferred history. To what extent my uncle, C. Henry Smith, had influenced me in this direction, I cannot say, but no doubt some. I had always looked up to and admired him as a favorite uncle. The superintendent at Midland, Michigan, formerly at St. Johns, offered me a job, but as I recall, I would have had to teach more English than history and social studies. I therefore opted for a positon at Walnut Creek, Holmes County, Ohio, even though it was a smaller school and offered less salary than the Midland positon.

In the meantime however new developments were occurring at Goshen. Professor Guy F. Hershberger felt that Goshen needed more help in the history department, and recommended to the administration that I be asked to get graduate training in history with the view of returning to my alma mater to teach. Both Dean Noah Oyer and President Sanford C. Yoder agreed with Hershberger's recommendation and invited me to return to teach history after securing my master's degree. After giving the matter serious consideration, I decided to accept the Goshen offer. According to my recollection, I had not as yet signed a contract for Walnut Creek. Since Milt had qualifications very similar to mine, I recommended him for the position. The Holmes County school officials, including Ivan Hostetler the principal, accepted the recommendation, and matters worked out very well all around.

In the meantime, Tim had accepted a similar position at Low Point, Illinois, near our old home.

For me the decision to prepare for teaching history at Goshen was one of the more significant ones that I have made.

CHAPTER 7

Ann Arbor 1928-1929

Choosing a graduate school in 1928 was not difficult for me. I completed college with a considerable debt, so financial considerations were important. The University of Michigan was a logical choice. It was close to Goshen and close to our home in Michigan where we still had our farm. Since I was still considered a Michigan resident the tuition fee was quite moderate. In addition Michigan had a reputation as a quality institution. With professors Van Tyne, Phillips, Cross, and others, the history department ranked high academically. So Michigan was the choice.

Finances were a problem but not an insurmountable obstacle. Goshen was willing to wait for payments on my college debt until I returned to teach. Mother Smith also helped me out with low-interest loans, as did C. S. (Grandpa) Schertz who was now living with his son and daughter-in-law in Goshen and was a supporter of higher education in the Mennonite Church.

Since Goshen College in 1928 was not yet accredited by the North Central Association I did not know what to expect in registering at the university in June. I had heard of cases where students had been docked some credits when taking a Goshen transcript to other institutions. But I was pleased to learn that I was accepted in the graduate school without condition.

The university required graduate students to select a minor as well as a major field of study. Thinking that political science would serve well, I selected it to go along with my history major. For my 1928 summer school courses I registered for Frayermuth's "French Revolution," Hirsch's "Economic and Social History of the American Colonies," and "Eighteenth Century

Europe" under professor Dutcher.

During the following academic year, 1928-1929, came the real "meat-and-potato" courses that I was fondly anticipating, especially those by C. H. Van Tyne and U. B. Phillips. Canadians are not always correct in their criticism of Americans south of the border always getting a wrong view of Canadian and British history. Van Tyne had done much to correct the distortion. He was one of the leading authorities on the causes of the American Revolutionary War and the relation of the Loyalists or Tories to it. In fact his school texts on American history were thought by some Americans to be too pro-British, so much so by Mayor Bill Thompson of Chicago that Van Tyne's texts were among those consigned to the fire burning ceremony which the mayor conducted on the shores of Lake Michigan earlier in the 1920s. So I enjoyed immensely both semesters of Van Tyne's "Political and Constitutional Development of the United States, 1763 to 1850."

By 1928 Ulrich B. Phillips had also established his reputation as an outstanding revisionist historian, in this case of American Negro slavery. Born and reared as a bourbon in Georgia, Phillips spent most of his adult life in the North, but remained rather defensive of his former section and its way of life. But that was not so unusual for the 1920s, for by that time even the North took a much less stringent view of the South, slavery, the Civil War, and even tended to go along with the South in condemning the Radical Republicans and the carpetbag governments they helped establish. Phillips took his graduate work at Columbia University where Professor William A. Dunning was attracting young southern historians because of his revisionist views on the Civil War and Reconstruction. The fact that Dunning was a northerner (from New Jersey) made his views doubly attractive to those whose parents and grandparents had fought in the "lost cause."

It was with pleasure therefore that I signed up for Phillips' courses on the antebellum South. I am glad that I took his courses and thus got the authentic, prevailing southern view. But in my judgment Phillips is a good example of those professors who were renowned research scholars but poor teachers. During the second semester he spent much of the time in class reading from the manuscript of his book which was in press—*Life and Labor in the Old South*—and published later in the year (1929). One mistake I possibly made, and discovered too late, was to take Phillips' seminar instead of Van Tyne's. The latter was geared more for those just starting their research. However, Phillips' field interested me more than Van Tyne's, and so possibly I gained as much as, if not more than, I lost. Even though I was rather pro-southern in my sympathies in the 1920s, I discovered in Phillips' seminar that I could not go as far as he did in defending the South. In my seminar report on President Polk and the causes of the Mexican War I was led to the conclusion that it was Polk's aggressive action and excessive claims in the disputed boundary area and his desire for California rather than the annexation of Texas and unpaid claims by Mexico which brought on the war. I still believe the same today. But Phillips was not happy that this young upstart in his seminar should question the views of the high and mighty, like Justin H. Smith and others, including himself, who justified United States action in Mexico 1846-1848.

Undoubtedly Phillips made an important contribution to American historiography by his careful study of plantation records—and not only the harsher state statutes—to show the actual conditions of the life of

Negro slaves. There is probably much truth in his conclusion in his classic *American Negro Slavery* that the "government of slaves was for the ninety and nine by men, and only for the hundredth by laws." There is also much validity in his emphasis that the central theme of southern history is that the South shall remain a white man's country; that before the Civil War slavery was a means to keep it so, and that after slavery other means were used to maintain the same end.

I learned much from Phillips' courses and his writings, as well as from discussions with fellow members in his classes. But I had to learn much more in later years as this memoir will indicate. I had to learn that segregation, which Phillips defended and even practiced in his class, was all wrong—dead wrong. That does not mean that I defended it particularly in the 1920s, but I certainly did not oppose it like I should have and did later. I had to learn that the so-called Progressive Movement from about 1900 to the 1920s was anything but progressive for the Blacks. It was a shameful progression backwards which made the fourteenth and fifteenth amendments to the constitution dead phrases and ghastly reminders of the lost battle for black freedom and equality. This is well illustrated by the dedication in 1923 of the beautiful memorial in Washington to the great emancipator, Abraham Lincoln, where Republican President Warren G. Harding spoke to an audience in which the Blacks were segregated!

No doubt others in Phillips' class also changed their views in later years. I know of no one who changed more radically than did Dwight L. Dumond. I sat next to him in class. He was more pro-southern than I was in the first place, and later became a very strong advocate for the Blacks. Dumond became Phillips' successor at Michigan. Very probably Phillips would have turned over in his grave had he heard what his succesor was telling his audiences about the Blacks, slavery, and civil rights!

In 1965, noting the world-wide revolution, he said that "neither force, nor fear, nor argument will stop this surge of masses of people for control of their own destiny." The only way in which the United States could redeem democracy and regain the respect of the world, he stated, was by "a monumental act of retributive justice." New attitudes and new practices are necessary "and inescapable," but that is not enough. We can, he continued, break down the barrier to communication between the races, convince the world of our sincerity, strengthen our nation, and recover some of what we have lost by oppression; "we can do all of these things and more by giving to every child of color the finest possible education and technical training at national expense, and never count the cost."

Dumond concluded that we could never *give* the Blacks anything for:

"Everything we ever do for them will bear the indelible mark of retribution. We can not repair the damage done, nor recall our acts of cruelty, but we can lighten the punishment on the day of judgment by matching every lynching of the past with a Ph.D. of the future . . . no nation can ever expect to recover its moral values by simply saying it is sorry. If its sorrow is deep enough to be lasting, it must entail more than lip-service to virtue."

What an irony that these statements should come from a student and successor of U. B. Phillips!

Another course in American history, my major interest, should be mentioned. This was Carter Goodrich's "American Economic Development". Here I got a good introduction to Frederick Jackson

Turner. Goodrich had us buy Turner's book, *The Frontier in American History*. Of the thousands of books I accumulated during my teaching and research career, this is one of the few I still have left. It is a historic, classic volume, and I felt it was worth retaining. At that time Goodrich was something of a Turnerian, as most historians in the American field were. Later, after he moved to Columbia University he became a mild, constructive critic of the Turner thesis and probably helped correct some distortions, for which Turner's disciples were responsible more than Turner himself.

At that time Michigan did not require a thesis for the M.A. The seminar course met the requirement. Quite a few term papers for courses were also required. I found research in the huge university library, for these term papers as well as for the seminar, a delightful experience.

Preparation for and attending classes of course was not the whole of university experience. But due to limited finances, my social life was limited. There was no Mennonite church or fellowship in Ann Arbor then, and so I attended various churches. I did discover some kindred religious spirits on the campus, especially graduates from Calvin College in Grand Rapids. Occasionally we met together to discuss issues growing out of the then current movements of Fundamentalism, Modernism and Liberalism.

Occasionally I attended the Mennonite church in Detroit where my cousin Elsie Smith King and her husband Clarence lived. Clarence was pastor of the church. Occasionally also I went home to St. Johns over weekends. In order to save money, I usually hitchhiked and had pretty good luck. During one period of my study in Ann Arbor—I have forgotten just when it was—I traveled more often to St. Johns. The Bethel congregation, my home church, had asked me to teach a singing class there, and in an unguarded moment I consented. I am not sure I should have done it, for my knowledge of music was not that great. I fear that my need for a few extra dollars might have had some influence on my decision. But we had a lot of fun during that period, and I don't think I did anybody any harm. And I hope I did not take money under false pretenses.

Extra-curricular activities on the campus, besides church-going, included attending some very good lectures and concerts. A few of the more noteworthy were Lowell Thomas (Sr.) who spoke on "With Lawrence in Arabia," and Oswald Garrison Villard, grandson of the famous abolitionist, William Lloyd Garrison, and son of the railroad builder in the Pacific northwest. Another lecture, which has proved very helpful to me throughout the years, was given by a Lutheran scholar who knew his theology and science. I don't remember the exact title but the address had to do with science and religion (or theology). I remember the main thrust. Yes, there sometimes is a conflict between science, which is what man thinks of nature, and theology, which is what man thinks of God. Since both science and theology are man-made formulas there can easily and likely be conflicts. But there is no conflict between nature and God who is the author of nature. Two of the concerts were by the young Vladimir Horowitz, pianist, and the Prague Teachers Male Chorus.

Michigan is known for its athletics, especially its football teams. I am not a great football fan, but since for some cause or other the tickets for that particular sport were free (rather included in the fees one paid) I attended the home games. Maybe one reason the tickets were free was that the authorities wanted to fill their huge new stadium. I am sorry that I was (and am) not enough of a fan to remember who the heroes (if any) on the team were that year, nor do I remember who our opponents were. I do remember eating at times in the same restaurant in which the coaches ate—Oosterbaan and others.

One episode during midyear almost changed my plans just a bit. In the fall of 1928 I joined the University Placement Bureau. It cost nothing and I thought I might as well have it available in case I ever should want to use it. I was surprised in January 1929 when the placement bureau called me and asked whether I wanted to teach history in the Ann Arbor High School beginning the second semester. I went down to talk it over with the high school authorities, and did consider the matter. With two summers at the University, it appeared that I could have taught at the high school and still have secured my master's by August 1929. But after thinking it over further, I decided to turn down the offer and get as much graduate work as possible before starting to teach at Goshen in September 1929.

CHAPTER 8
A Pup Instructor at Goshen College/University of Chicago 1929-1935

The five or six weeks of teaching Music I at Hesston College in the fall of 1921 hardly qualified to make me an experienced teacher. Since I was therefore a new teacher and as such had to prepare all new courses, Dean Noah Oyer was kind to me and had me teach only four subjects: United States history, European history, political and constitutional history of U.S. for upper classmen, and American government. Beginning teachers today would consider such a load slavery. But we did not know any better then, worked hard, and somehow made it—to the not-too-great detriment of the students, we hope. The second semester was the same, except that state and local government took the place of American Government.

The year of 1929 was a unique one in which to start a forty-three year teaching career. I had taught very little more than a month when the worst panic and depression in history broke upon the country. Fortunately, I have never been able to discover any cause-and-effect relationship between the two events! Be that as it may stock prices on the exchanges plummeted for years with only occasional and brief changes in the trend, despite President Hoover's recurring pleas "not to sell America short" and his frequent plaintive proclamation that "prosperity was just hovering around the corner." This was soon translated by critics into "prosperity was just 'Hoovering' around the corner."

The tremendous drop in stock prices was simply symptomatic of prices in general. All kinds of adjustments had to be made. Deflation was now the problem and governments worked at the problem of halting the downward trend. Faculty salaries, always low, had to be cut still lower. Students often had to pay at least part of their bills in notes, which were then used in part to pay faculty salaries. These were difficult times, especially for those of us who were just starting to teach and still had school debts to pay. My more than $3000 debt was a large amount for that time. But I had helpful, sympathetic creditors: mother, Grandpa Schertz, and Goshen College. And our college community was a close-knit, sharing and caring one, ready to help each other when necessary. In fact most of the faculty had been my teachers when I was a student.

I lived in the newly-constructed J. S. Coffman Hall the first year I taught, and that was not expensive. But living with those students was an experience! It wasn't quite like it was one time when C. F. Derstine held evangelistic meetings at the college and lived part of the time in the men's dormitory. He said living there reminded him of heaven: "There was no night there." But occasionally I did have to remind students that they were getting a little noisy. I do remember how my good friend Orie Eigsti and his roommate, who lived directly above me, needed a little fatherly advice once or twice about noise, and upon hearing me tap on the ceiling or the pipes they became perfect gentlemen. It is possible that Orie had an additional incentive to heed my advice. He was taking one of my history courses!

In those days I was young and agile. To prove it, let facts be submitted to a candid world. I ate my meals in the college dining room which was in Kulp Hall barely a block from Coffman. A warning bell would ring ten minutes before the breakfast bell. I could sleep until that first bell rang, then get up, shave, wash and dress and get over to the dining room in time for the breakfast prayer!

Coffman Hall served me very well, but throughout that first year I was looking forward to something still better—marriage. After graduating from college in

1928, Verna resumed teaching in the elementary grades—this time at Sterling, Illinois. The wedding date was September 3, 1930 at Verna's home near Noble, Iowa. The happy occasion was saddened by the fact that father Graber was very ill with cancer and had to remain in bed during the ceremony. But he was glad to see this long-awaited event finally occur before his passing which was only a few weeks away. So we made the wedding a simple one, with some of the relatives not being there because of the illness. Simon Gingerich, bishop at the Sugar Creek Church where Verna was a member, officiated at the wedding.

We took our honeymoon on the installment plan—also because of father Graber's illness. The first installment was to Goshen with a stopover in Chicago. On later installments we took the traditional trip to Niagra Falls, and elsewhere.

In Goshen we started housekeeping in the newly-remodeled North Hall (College) apartments. The college had moved East Hall, a men's dormitory, to the north side of College Avenue, renamed it North Hall, and later made it into apartments. We lived here from September 1930 to January 1935. The first days here were not easy for us, especially for Verna. We knew that we could expect a call from Noble any day about father's passing. The call came September 24, three weeks after our wedding.

After returning to Goshen and resuming teaching, it was not very long until we had to face another illness—this time in our academic family. Dean Noah Oyer became ill with typhoid fever in December 1930. Not considered too serious at first, the illness lingered on into February and, in spite of what seemed adequate medical care, became a matter of great concern. By his untimely passing February 25, 1931—he was only

39—the entire Mennonite brotherhood lost an important reconciling influence.

In 1931 my brother George finished grade school in Michigan, and George, mother and I decided to have him come to Goshen for his high school. George was only seven years old when father died. Naturally concerned about him, father had asked me to help mother look after George, and I promised I would. So Verna and I were happy to have him come to Goshen, and be of whatever help we could to him. Part of the time he stayed with us, but most of the time he lived in a college dormitory under the care of the dormitory officials as other college students. He did well in high school, liked it, and played on the football team. After graduating from Goshen High School he remained for two years of college and then transferred to Michigan State at East Lansing for training in agriculture. After spending over four years in Civilian Public Service in World War II George and Wilma Miller from Fulton County, Ohio, whom he married during the war, became farmers near Eureka and then St. Johns, Michigan. Wilma also taught school for many years. In addition they reared three fine boys all of whom have families today. It was always comforting to the rest of us to know that at least one member of the family remained a son of the soil and continued the old family tradition of farming.

To come back to my educational career at Goshen. Before I started teaching I had decided that I definitely needed more graduate work and would get it as soon as possible. So in the summers of 1930, 1931, and 1932 I attended the University of Chicago and secured the equivalent of a full academic year of training. Taking mostly advanced courses in American history and a few in American government and in Latin American history, I found the experience at Chicago a rewarding one and a definite help in my teaching. I had earlier planned to shoot for the Ph.D. and thought I might do so in Chicago. But those plans changed.

In the meantime I enjoyed all my courses, some more than others of course. It would be boring to mention all of them, but I must point out a few. Two of them under Professor Marcus Jernegan were in the fields of American historiography, and historical method and criticism. Jernegan had gotten his doctorate at the University of Chicago—in fact he had remembered Uncle C. Henry Smith as a fellow student—and emphasized the importance of the historian striving to attain the scientific-objective goal of "telling the truth, the whole truth and nothing but the truth." He realized it was not possible to attain these fully, given our human weaknesses and limitations, but he emphasized that we should not use these limitations as excuses for not vigorously training and disciplining ourselves to be as truthful and objective as possible. Otherwise we would have prostituted history that would be slanted and unreliable. I always appreciated this kind of training that I got under Jernegan, and others of course. I did not have to go quite as far as he did when he said, "you can't believe anything strongly and be a good historian." I felt that for me as a Christian who had values there was no conflict with the historian's goal of telling the truth and only the truth, for that was also the goal of the Christian.

I enjoyed also taking work under Professor William E. Dodd on reconstruction of the South, and of the North as he emphasized. It was interesting to compare him with U. B. Phillips at the University of Michigan. Dodd was also a Southerner, having been born and reared in North Carolina. Both of them were great authorities on the South. But Dodd was more liberal in his social philosophy and less defensive of the South and its way of life. Since I had been seriously considering getting my doctorate in history at Chicago and had wanted to study under Dodd it was unfortunate for me that he left the university in 1933 and became President Franklin D. Roosevelt's ambassador to Germany.

Problems in Central American Diplomacy under Quincy Wright was also profitable, as was American Cultural History under Merle Curti. Adding to the pleasures of my Chicago experience was the fact that I had relatives and other friends living in the area. The first summer (1929) I roomed with my cousins, Frank and Laura Smith King. Each one was my first cousin, and I had always felt close to them and their families. Art Smith, Laura's brother, also roomed there. I attended church with them on Sundays at the Chicago Home Mission, where another cousin, Emma Oyer, was a worker for many years. Part of our ritual each weekday evening was to come downstairs and listen over radio to hear "Amos and Andy" tell about their activities for the day, especially with their "Fresh Air Taxicab Company." Years later this program was not considered acceptable for airing. But at that time we were not conscious of any dislike for the program that the Blacks might have had.

In the summer of 1931 I roomed in a fraternity house that was not serving as such during the summer and was being rented out for the purpose of bringing in some extra dollars. The following summer I roomed at Arthur Slagel's. Arthur was from Flanagan, Illinois, and was one of my teachers at Hesston. A graduate of Goshen, he had married Vesta Zook, also a Goshen graduate. Both of them had done relief work in the Near East. Ezra Camp and I were roommates that summer.

There were various reasons why the summer of 1932 turned out to be my last quarter at Chicago. Others in addition to Professor Dodd left the university about this time. The coming of Robert Maynard Hutchins in 1929 as president and his inauguration of a program which quite a few thoroughly disliked caused a tremendous furor among the faculty. Hutchins' program was the conversation piece of many faculty groups, and they pulled no punches in saying what they thought about it. At one of these faculty groups one upset faculty member was telling another what he thought of Hutchins. The lady listened for some time and then asked the gentleman: "Do you know who I am?" "No, I don't," said the man. "Well, I am Mrs. Hutchins!" Startled, the faculty member asked: "Do you know who I am?" "No, I don't," replied Mrs. Hutchins. The gentleman responded: "Thank God!" and departed posthaste. The story is supposed to be true. But whether true or not, a number of faculty members, including some historians, did leave. Another reason I left was financial. In the early thirties the depression was getting worse rather than better, and in those rough times I thought I could finance my program better at a place like Indiana University, which had a department of American history that looked very good to me.

Not only did I feel that I should get more graduate training in order to be a good teacher, I felt also the need to travel more—especially in America since my first interest was American history. During the spring break in 1932, I accepted the invitation of Frank and Laura King of Chicago to travel to Washington D.C. with them and their two children, Edith and Harold. As a teacher of American history and government I thought that of all places I ought to have first hand experience with our national capitol and its goings-on. But I was still too young and innocent then to appreciate what someone said later about Washington:

"Washington is a city in which truth is a scarce commodity. Politicians therefore use it very sparingly." Or that other gag about a father and his young son visiting Congress. The son asked his father whether the chaplain prays for the members of congress. "No, son," said the father. "The chaplain comes into the room, looks over the congressmen, and then prays for his country." Or that one from Bismarck: "If you like sausages and legislation, stay away from where they are made."

All joking aside, I enjoyed my stay in Washington. I spent most of my time visiting Congress and the Supreme Court. The Kings had an appointment to meet President Hoover, and I was invited to go along. I declined, however, having decided that visiting the Supreme Court probably would have more educational value for me at that time than meeting the President. Also of interest and value to me was to go in the evenings to the lobbies of the hotels where Congressmen stayed, and sit around and listen to them discuss politics and strategy. I remember especially sitting near and listening to John Nance Garner from Texas, who was then Speaker of the House. He became Franklin D. Roosevelt's running mate in the election of 1932.

It was my good fortune to attend two sessions of the Democratic convention in Chicago in the summer of 1932. Since I was attending the University of Chicago at the time, I did not have to make a special trip to the city. But there was such a demand for tickets of admission to the convention that securing them was a big problem. I had thought, however, that I had the problem solved. An old politician from Goshen (Mr. Beane), who had lived in Idaho many years ago and had served on the Democratic National Committee, promised me that because of these old connections he could and would get me a ticket. I was to meet him at a certain place and time. But when I went there, no Mr. Beane was to be found!

I then went to the hotel where the Indiana delegation was staying and sought out Bob Proctor of Elkhart, one of the leading delegates. Bob told me there were no tickets, but gave me a slip of paper with Mayor (of Chicago) Cermak's name on it and said that would let me in. With hopes renewed, I happily went to the stadium, the site of the convention. My hopes sagged when they would not let me in at the first entrance I tried. The result at the second entrance was similar, except that the official there told me to what entrance to go for admission with that paper. It worked! To my surprise the hall was not nearly filled and the audience was being entertained by Amos and Andy. The next order of business was the presentation of the platform, but that committee was not quite ready to report. In just a short time the chairman announced that the convention was adjourned, to meet again that evening!

Back at the university, when I was telling some of my classmates my experiences of the morning, one asked me whether I would like to attend the following evening. It didn't take me long to say yes. She was a student from Georgia who had a ticket she was unable to use that night. The session I attended then proved a memorable one. It met all night. With an excellent seat in front near the speaker's stand, elevated enough that one could see what was going on anywhere in the auditorium, I had the time of my life; and what an education it was! They had the nominating speeches and parades which consumed the time up until about two or three o'clock in the morning. These parades were interesting to me because on the ''inside'' I got a closer view of their ''spontaneity'' than one got over radio or later over T.V. Senator Alben Barkley of Kentucky came to the area where I was sitting to talk with some friends and urged them to come down to the main floor to participate in a parade that they were going to have in a few minutes. (I think the parade was for Roosevelt.)

At the conclusion of the speeches and parades, the Roosevelt forces, which were in command of the convention, pulled a surprise on their opponents, especially those who were working for Alfred E. Smith. Somewhere around two or three a.m. they started balloting when apparently Roosevelt's opponents thought there would be none until later that day. Some of these had retired for the night. Caught off guard, the anti-Roosevelt forces still at the convention engaged in all kinds of stalling tactics while calling their delegates in the hotels to come at once to cast their votes. Before long I saw them returning, some of them, it appeared, dressed in their pajamas and bath robes. Eventually completed, the first ballot showed Roosevelt far ahead, but short of the two-thirds necessary at that time for the nomination. The second ballot showed a little increase in his vote, and the third still more.

At that point, which was already dawn, the Roosevelt forces, led by Jim Farley, again surprised the audience by calling for adjournment until that evening. People were suspicious that something dramatic was shortly to happen; and it did during the day. When the convention reconvened that evening only one more ballot was necessary. A deal had been made between the Roosevelt and John Nance Garner forces. Garner, who controlled the Texas and California delegates, threw his support to F.D.R., and that was enough to nominate him. Only one ballot was necessary for the vice-presidency. It was John Nance Garner.

The ensuing election campaign was an exciting one, especially for the Democrats, because it appeared that they had the best chance for success since 1916, if not

1912. Roosevelt had an engaging personality, a fine radio voice, and a family name that did not hurt him. I remember talking to an Iowa farmer before the election. I asked him for whom he was going to vote. He replied: "Well his father [meaning Theodore] made a good president and I think Franklin will too." He mistakenly thought Franklin was Theodore's son! How many others made the same mistake we have no way of knowing.

But the chief thing that F.D.R. had going for him was the greatest depression in U.S. history. And poor Herbert Hoover unjustly got all the blame for it. Many of the more progressive Republicans, especially the followers of Theodore Roosevelt, one after another announced for F.D.R. One of the last of these was Hiram Johnson of California, who was Teddy's running mate in 1912. So it was pretty clear long before November that Hoover would be overwhelmingly defeated in 1932, as he was overwhelmingly elected in 1928.

We duly discussed the results in our American history class. Members took the election seriously, and were ready to defend one side or the other. We had agreed before hand that the members of the party that lost would provide the refreshments for the class discussion meeting after the election. "A good [and profitable] time was had by all."

One activity which I felt was necessary for college teachers—and especially for a young, developing one—was to join his professional organizations, read their journals, and attend their meetings. The first one I attended was the meeting of the American Historical Association in 1931 in Minneapolis. The presidential address by Carl Becker, entitled "Everyman His Own Historian," was one of the most stimulating I have ever heard or read. It was always included in the required readings for our history majors when I later taught the history seminar in historical method and criticism. I attended many of our professional meetings throughout the years, on the national and state level. One other notable one in the early years was in 1933 at Urbana-Champaign, Illinois, where the famous Charles A. Beard delivered a somewhat controversial presidential address on "Written History as an Act of Faith." This was at the depth of the great depression while Roosevelt's New Deal was being put into effect. Some thought Beard was leaning too far in the direction of socialism and also was ready to swing too far away from the ideal or goal of objective history. I tended to agree with those who expressed this concern.

Along about 1933 and 1934 Verna and I made two brief trips into the South. I was much interested also in this section of the country—having studied it considerably in my courses under U. B. Phillips at the University of Michigan—and I thought I ought to see it firsthand.

Mary Royer, a teaching colleague, wanted to attend a teachers' convention in Nashville, and so we were glad to take her and one of her students along.

At that time the area was the old segregated South. One episode stands out in memory and made a tremendous impression on me. The dinner for the convention—which was the only session that Verna and I attended—was held on the campus of a state college for Blacks. Protocol demanded that some official from the institution welcome the people to the campus. The Black president of the Black college did this very acceptably and graciously. But the thing which hit home to me was the fact that he could welcome the group there but could not remain to eat with them on his own campus because they were white!! This was an important episode in opening my eyes to the ridiculousness of racial segregation and in strengthening my determination to help make equality of races more than dead letters in our Declaration of Independence and Constitution of the United States.

The year following (1934), also during the spring break, Verna and I traveled as far south as eastern Florida and New Orleans to have first hand experience with the deep South. Ethel and S. A. Yoder, professor of English, and Verna's sister, Elizabeth Graber, accompanied us.

My teaching load was quite heavy during these years. It was not made lighter when I was asked in 1932 to serve also as dean of men. I taught fifteen or sixteen hours a week—actually seventeen one or two years—served as dean of men, was a member of four or five faculty committees, and had no secretary! I always felt more sorry for the students than I did for myself. Fortunately this condition continued only until 1935 when I secured a leave of absence to complete my work for the doctorate.

One innovation I introduced as dean of men, I felt, deserved a longer trial period than it received. This had to do with the perennial question of required chapel attendance. I believed in required chapel attendance, but I believed in making a difference in the application between lower and upper classmen. The requirement remained the same for freshmen and sophomores. For juniors I recommended—and the faculty accepted—a system of allowing a few cuts each semester, for which absences no explanation was necessary. For seniors I recommended—and faculty accepted—dropping the attendance requirement altogether, but urging attendance on other grounds. My philosophy was that though college students were not mature (indeed when do we become mature?), college age ought to be a period in which young people continue to grow toward that goal, and in which they ought to exercise more self discipline and responsibility as adults; and that certainly seniors ought to be closer to that goal than freshmen. These new rules, I thought, worked quite well during the short period I continued as dean of men before leaving. But when I returned two and a half years later the old requirements had been reinstituted. I never did find out why.

In the summer of 1934 it was our delightful privilege to travel extensively in the West. Cousin Art Smith, a high school biology teacher in South Bend, joined Verna and me on this journey. This was the first of a number of trips that Art took with us. He was an excellent traveling companion. He added a scientific dimension which was helpful, and became as enthusiastic about the historic aspects as I was. There is an old saying that if you travel with someone and you are as good friends at the end of the journey as at the beginning you are friends for life. Art and we traveled some 50,000 or 60,000 miles together, and, if anything, were even better friends at the end. Most of this traveling was in the West where my teaching interest was the strongest.

We made the trip in the new Chevrolet we had purchased the year before. Bought in March 1933 when all the banks were closed, the purchase price of $485 indicated the prevailing desperate times. The Miller brothers in Goshen were accustomed to making as good deals for their patrons as possible, and at this time were willing to go the limit. They had on hand their best model, a four-door, six cylinder, that they offered for $500. I happened to have a check for $485—I don't remember where I got it—which I laid before them and said I could give that amount for the car. They took it even though it was the first time they had ever sold a new car for less than $500. The car proved very adequate for our trip even though we had to fasten the luggage on one of the running boards and on a rack in the back. To cut down our costs we often cooked our simple meals on a small gas stove we took with us, and occasionally some of us would sleep in the car.

We wanted to see the northwest, the Pacific coast, California, and the southwest. Since we traveled during the last of July and most of August, we thought it wise to go west during the peak of the hot season by way of the cooler northern route, and then return from California by way of the hotter southern route after the hottest weather had passed. But we missed it. Our hottest weather was in South Dakota where the thermometer indicated 114 in the shade—and no shade. At Chamberlain Verna passed out. But we had just gotten to a restaurant, and some fans, coffee, and some ice brought her back. Farther west in the state, as the elevation gradually increased, the weather became more bearable. But it was a rough day. And 1934 was a hot, dry year. At Mitchell, where the famous Corn Palace is located, corn had tasseled that was little more than a foot high. As one farmer told us, the area that year "would not have enough corn to feed a she-wolf." Dead trees and even dead cattle were common sights. One thing I learned from that and later trips in the West and in Latin America was that altitude was more important than latitude in determining comfortable weather.

We called this 1934 trip our introduction to the West, and agreed we would later want to take a longer, more advanced course on the area. As it turned out we took quite a few more. To summarize, we found the Badlands and especially the Black Hills to be all that we had expected, and the Big Horn Mountains—of which we had heard less—more than anticipated. One of the anticipated highlights of course was Yellowstone Park. There are in the U.S. numerous fine national parks, and they are hard to compare because they differ considerably. But Yellowstone has an amazing variety of beauty and outstanding attractions. I have seen it a number of times; but the trouble with it in recent years is that it is cluttered up with too many people.

From Yellowstone we went south directly into the beautiful Grand Teton National Park, where the mountain scenery rivals that of the Canadian Rockies. From there we followed the Snake River in Idaho to Twin Falls where we made a brief visit in the home of old family friends of Verna, Dr. and Mrs. J. E. Langenwalter. For many years Dr. Langenwalter lived in Wayland, Iowa and was the Graber family doctor. During this brief visit Mrs. Langenwalter wanted to sing with us "Ich Weiss Einen Strom". It made such an impression on Art that we got copies of the song and sang it frequently while traveling. It was a supplement to "I Owe the Lord a Morning Song" which we used each morning as a devotional song.

From Twin Falls our route took us through Boise to Nampa, Idaho where we visited old school friends from Hesston and Goshen days, especially the Dr. Hostetler family, with whom we stayed one or two nights. We had gotten acquainted with Vertie, Leo, and Adelia in school.

From Nampa we headed for Oregon by way of Pendleton and the Columbia River. For many years I had heard of the scenic highway along the Columbia River. We were anxious to see it, and we were not disappointed. The farther we proceeded toward Portland the more beautiful the route became. But Portland was not our stopping place—rather Albany in the Willamette Valley where Verna had some relatives and friends who had formerly lived in Wayland, Iowa. Mrs. Sam Kennel was a first cousin and Verna also had some Roth cousins there.

We stayed with the Kennels over a weekend and attended the Fairview church with them on Sunday. Either on Saturday or Monday Sam showed us how farming by his large combine was carried on in Oregon. On that point they were a little ahead of us in Indiana and Illinois. On another point they were not ahead of us—at least Art didn't think so. The Kennels were modernizing their country home when we were there and had some ditches dug in the yard. So to go to the "rest room" we had to go outside. This offered a few problems at nighttime. One was to keep the dogs from announcing the fact to the world, and the other was to keep from falling into one of the ditches! Art failed on the latter! Fortunately there were no casualties.

We enjoyed immensely our visit with the Kennels and others at Albany. From there we headed for the famous Crater Lake, about which Art had been preaching to us for weeks. He would say, "Bill, they say that if you take a good look at Crater Lake you will be a changed person." And of course he meant for the better. So we had to see Crater Lake. We wanted to be changed for the better! Well, Art was right. One cannot see, and meditate on, the magnificent handiwork of God and not be a better person. The same was true of those gigantic, inspiring redwoods in northern California, and of Yosemite National Park where we spent several days. Enroute we were amply rewarded by visiting the historic sites in San Fransisco. From Yosemite we continued south to Fresno, Bakersfield, and Los Angeles, more specifically Venice on the ocean where Verna's uncle Jake Conrad and wife Ruth lived, together with daughter Lois.

We stayed with the Conrads for several days. They were excellent hosts and did a fine job of showing us around. Lois, as I recall, even went along with us to

Clockwise from above: John J. Smith, father of Willard Smith, in his early 20's (photo taken mid-1890's). Born 1874, died 1924.; Katie (Smith) Smith, Willard's mother, at 20 years. Born 1879, died 1914.; Willard H. Smith at a young and innocent age.

Clockwise from top left: Maternal grandfather John Smith, 1860's (later Bishop in Metamora, Illinois); Paternal grandfather Peter Smith; Verna Graber's family in the early 1920's. **Front:** Lena, Daniel, Fannie, Esther. **Back:** Katie, Verna [later Smith], C.L., Mary, Elizabeth, Joseph D., Anna.

Above: "Stuck in the mud along the Santa Fe Trail" near Trinidad, Colorado, 1914. **From left:** Milton Smith, John J. Smith, Mary Grove (second from right). The other women are Abbie Roupp and Ida Kreider. **Right:** Hesston College's Apollo Quartet, 1917-18: Stanley Brubaker (Ontario), Willard H. Smith (Goshen), Edward Yoder (Kalona, Iowa), Chris (C.L.) Graber (Wayland, Iowa).

Above: At the Half-way house on Pike's Peak. We walked half way, then took the cog railroad. **From left:** Emma Eby [later Hershey], Keturah Kauffman [later Dreier and Buckwalter], Willard Smith, Ben J. Schertz (Willard's uncle through marriage), and Tilman (Tim) Smith. Summer 1914. **Left:** Brothers at the Smith family home, St. Johns, Michigan, about 1924-25. **From left:** Milton, George, Willard, Tilman.

Clockwise from top left: Willard Smith and Verna Graber on their wedding day, September 3, 1930, in Noble, Iowa; Joseph D. Graber, one of my very close friends, and Willard Smith, Goshen, 1950's; Willard and Verna at Pawnee Rock in western Kansas, 1941. There's an old saying among the Pawnee Indians, "If you love on Pawnee Rock you'll love forever."

Above: MCC workers in the Chaco, Paraguay, 1945. **From left:** Vernon Schmidt, Sarah (Histand) Schmidt, Waldo Hiebert, Rachel Hiebert, Orval Myers, Clara Schmidt, Dr. John Schmidt (holding John Jr.), Dr. A.M. Lohrentz, Willard H. Smith. *Photo by Vernon Schmidt.* **Left:** "Listening" to the New York Philharmonic on a Sunday afternoon, 1940's.

Above: Willard Smith with Goshen College Lecture-Music Series guest Carl Sandburg, 1953. **Right:** Sandburg's inscription in Willard's copy of Sandburg's *The People, Yes.*

For Willard H. Smith
and his kith and kin :
may all weathers be
kind :

Carl Sandburg
Oct. 18   1953
Goshen, Indiana

Clockwise from top left: Eating our supper at famous South Pass in the Rockies (Wyoming), 1947. **From left:** Willard Smith, Art Smith, Esther Graber, Verna Smith. Sculptor Mahonri Young (center, grandson of Brigham), in front of his (and my) favorite plaque on "This is the Place Monument" near Salt Lake City, Utah, 1947. With him are descendents of George and Tamsen Donner, in whose honor this plaque was made.; My best picture of ruts—near Guernsey, Wyoming. Art Smith points out the earliest wheel markings in sandstone from wagons heading west on the Oregon, California and Mormon Trails.

Above: A "typical classroom experience," late '50s at Goshen College. **Right:** The four GC presidents under whom Willard and Verna Smith served. **Seated:** Sanford C. Yoder (GC 1923-40), Ernest E. Miller (1940-54) **Standing:** J. Lawrence Burkholder (1971-84) and Paul E. Mininger (1954-71).

Above: A gathering on the occasion of Elizabeth Smith's 90th birthday, November 1976. **Couples from left:** George and Wilma (Miller) Smith, Tilman and Louella (Schertz) Smith, Milton and Betty (Twining) Smith, Lauren and Dorothy (Smith) Shank, Willard and Verna (Graber) Smith. **Left:** The Smith children with mother Elizabeth on her 90th birthday, **from left:** George, Dorothy, Tilman, Elizabeth, Willard, Milton.

Above: Tilman, Willard and Milton Smith—Retirement Days at Greencroft, Goshen. "Retirement 'ain't' easy—these unupholstered shovel handles leave much to be desired!" **Right:** James Earl Fraser's, "The End of the Trail" sculpture in Mooney Grove Park, Visalia, California. (Photo courtesy Albert's Studios, Visalia, Calif.)

Willard and Verna Smith on their 50th wedding anniversary,
September 3, 1980.

Catalina Island. She was willing to take time off from her work at Bank America. Among the many places visited was Knott's Berry Farm. Their famous berry pie has a way of sticking not only to your ribs, but to your memory! I wish I'd have a fresh piece of it now!

From L.A. we pointed our Chevy toward Grand Canyon and points east. Like the others, Grand Canyon National Park has a majesty and grandeur of its own and can't be compared with the rest. Meditating and viewing this gigantic scene over a period of time, watching the changing colors with the changing sun, inspires me to a degree that few scenes can equal. It is scenes like these and others in western America that pull me back again and again to fill my cup of inspiration when it needs to be filled!

Another stop worth mentioning was the visit to the Hopi Indian snake dance ceremonial on the Hopi reservation north of Holbrook, Arizona. In this ceremonial in which the Indians pray for rain, those participating take live rattle snakes in their mouths and perform dances. No picture taking was permitted. All cameras had to be checked at the entrance. A large crowd, including many tourists, were on hand to see the Indians dance with rattlers in their mouths and, they say, never get bitten. Mrs. Harold Ickes, the wife of Roosevelt's Secretary of Interior, was one of the visitors.

The next stop of any consequence was Colorado Springs and Manitou, Colorado. Here we stayed with Mrs. Hough whom we had known from former years. We saw the usual sights of interest including Seven Falls, where Helen Hunt Jackson's burro was still to be found. These falls of course are always beautiful. But I was struck with this remarkable burro. It had a way of defying time. It had (according to officials) the same age as in 1914 when I saw it the first time—about twenty-five years! Some burro!

The only other event I shall note is going up Pike's Peak in our car via the recently completed road. This contrasted interestingly with 1914 when we went up (most of the way) by cog railroad. This time we started early, between two and three a.m., because we wanted to see the sunrise from the peak. We had heard it was best not to eat breakfast first. But I did chew a piece of Black Jack gum. That proved to be a sad mistake! On the way up I began to develop belly cramps, and I began to search for a "rest room." But of course none was available. We must have been above the tree line when things "got serious." I couldn't even find a tree to hide behind. Then I began to look for rocks. I prayed for a rock, not to fall on me, but to hide me from my fellowmen. But I found none large enough to conceal my inner weakness. It came to the point where, rock or no rock, I had to stop. Period. Fortunately, no car passed during this traumatic event! So we proceded on our way to the top to enjoy a glorious sunrise. But I learned my lesson about how to prepare to go up Pike's Peak!

Resuming our way eastward, we stopped briefly at La Junta to visit Walter Schertzes, Clarence Ebersoles, and other old friends whom we had known at La Junta, Hesston, or Goshen.

I am not certain whether we stopped at Hutchinson to visit our King relatives there, but we probably did. I know we stopped at Hesston. Art always got a kick out of visiting at Uncle Sam Kings, as did the rest of us, enjoying uncle's sly humor and reminders to his guests how expensive the food was and how costly it was to entertain people!

Our last stop was Eureka, Illinois, where we left Art off and where we still had many relatives in 1934, including brother Tim and family in Roanoke. After visiting briefly in the area we went on to Goshen, "Home, Sweet Home."

The approximately five weeks for this adventure were very well spent. We all agreed that purposeful travel was education of a high order.

CHAPTER 9
Completing Graduate Work:
Indiana University 1935-1937

Even though purposeful travel was educational, I still had some formal academic training to complete for my Ph.D. I have indicated disappointment in the fact that William E. Dodd and some others left the University of Chicago. Another reason for selecting Indiana University was financial: the persistence of the depression and the thought that I could more likely get a teaching assistantship at Bloomington. This proved to be the case. In addition I.U. had a good department in history, especially American. Albert E. Kohlmeier, head of the history department, was my advisor at first. For my program I wanted to take more work in U.S. history than their program customarily permitted. Kohlmeier made this concession and allowed me to count early and recent American as two fields instead of one. But he would not permit me to use Spanish instead of French as one of my foreign languages, which Chicago would have permitted. So I took the traditional French and German. One had to have at least three fields in history. In addition to the two in American, I selected modern European, and government and economics. I chose modern (especially recent) European because it would complement and support my interest in recent American history, and also because F. Lee Benns was the well-known author of two widely-used texts in recent European history: *Europe Since 1914* and *Europe Since 1870*. At I.U., like Michigan and Chicago, some of the teachers were excellent, and others were mediocre. It so happened that Kohlmeier, head of the department, Ford Hall, head of the government department, and James Moffat, head of the economics department, were three of the best teachers I have had anywhere. R. C. Buley, Pulitzer prize winner with his two volumes on *The Old Northwest*, was also stimulating. William O. Lynch and John D. Barnhart were also good, as was F. Lee Benns in modern European. Oscar O. Winther, authority on the Far West, came to I.U. shortly before I left. Logan Esarey, authority on Indiana history and the Mid-West, was supposed to be my chief advisor. But because of an illness he contracted I did not have much work under him, and I ended up being directed in my program by a committee composed of Kohlmeier, Buley, Lynch, Benns, Hall, and Moffat.

Verna and I moved to Bloomington in January 1935, at the end of the first semester. I did not apply for a teaching job the second semester or for the following summer. But I did for the school year 1935-1936, and easily got one in American government. Since I had taught the course at Goshen the task was not difficult. The next year Kohlmeier wanted me to teach a class in American history, and I was glad to do that. But in January 1937 he surprised me by asking me to teach Esarey's two sections of Indiana history during the second semester of that year. Not feeling well prepared for that, I would have preferred to continue with American history. But because of Esarey's illness and Kohlmeier's strong plea, I consented to make the switch. The experience was a stimulating one for me, and I think the students learned some things about Indiana history. I *know* the teacher did.

I should have explained that Esarey was assigned as my chief advisor because of my dissertation topic: Schuyler Colfax of South Bend. Already at Chicago in talking with Professor Dodd about a possible dissertation topic, upon hearing I was from Goshen, Indiana, he immediately suggested two possibilities: Hugh Mc-Culloch of Ft. Wayne and Schuyler Colfax of South

Bend. Work ought to be done, he said, on both of these men. Because of prejudice in those days against Radical Republicans, I chose McCulloch and began to do some introductory work on him while still at Goshen. This included one or two trips to Ft. Wayne to talk with a grandson of McCulloch who had charge of his grandfather's papers located in the Lincoln Life Insurance Company building in that city. I was the first one to get permission to use these papers. Hence I was surprised at Bloomington—even after Kohlmeier and others had said it would be all right to work on McCulloch—to have William O. Lynch tell me that he was sorry, but one of his graduate students had already been assigned that topic for his dissertation. So I had to change to Colfax. In the end—even though the student assigned to McCulloch never completed his work—I was glad, as will be explained later, that I took up Colfax.

Life at Bloomington had a very pleasant dimension to it that it didn't have at Ann Arbor or Chicago. Verna was with me. When I was at Michigan we were not yet married, and during the three summer quarters at Chicago she was occupied elsewhere. In fact two of those summers she took graduate work at the University of Iowa.

At Bloomington we eventually found a nice apartment in a duplex house at 315 E. Smith Ave., near the University. Mrs. Nora Foster, a dear elderly lady who was blind, was the owner and lived in the other apartment. Not only our Mennonite belief in simplicity but economic considerations especially called for a simple life style. Since I fired the furnace and Verna read to her two hours a day for virtually nothing, Mrs. Foster rented the apartment to us at a low cost. Groceries also were not expensive. For some months in 1935 I kept account of our grocery expenses. Verna and I were able to live on $3.00 a week. We could even splurge at times and buy a good tender cubed steak for ten cents apiece. Prices of other household necessities were also reasonable. I bought a ten-inch electric oscillating fan for $5.00 and used it for forty years.

Since there was no Mennonite church in Bloomington, we decided to attend the congregations of various denominations and find out more about them. Mrs. Foster was a member of the Christian (Disciples) Church, and we attended there with her several times. For us Mennonites the interesting thing about the Church of Christ was its conservatism, particularly with regard to using no musical instruments in church worship. The Methodist Church experienced a fire while we were in Bloomington which gutted the building but left part of the tower and the cross still standing. At a meeting of the congregation the next Sunday in a University building the pastor preached a powerful sermon on ''The Cross Still Stands.'' In addition to the sermon at the Baptist Church, we attended a Sunday school class ably taught by my chief economics professor, James E. Moffat. At the Episcopal Church we worshipped with some of my other professors.

As to the other groups with which we worshipped, the Presbyterians had three different churches: the United, the Reformed, and the regular (Northern) Presbyterian. The Reformed was the most conservative of these three. The pastor told me their members do not vote in political elections, the chief reason being that the word God is not mentioned in the U.S. constitution.

The pastor of the regular Presbyterian congregation jokingly stated that Bloomington had the reputation of having three Presbyterian churches: the United, the Reformed, and one that was neither united nor reformed. Incidentally, Rev. Swartz of this regular

Presbyterian church preached one of the most powerful sermons against war that I have heard anywhere. The church that we attended probably more than any other was the Lutheran, a member of the Missouri Synod. The pastor and his wife, Rev. and Mrs. Stephan, became good friends of ours. In fact there were a number of things about the church that reminded us of the Mennonites—their conservatism, closed communion, not working too closely with other groups, frowning on card playing, et cetera. Despite this last point the Stephans taught Verna and me how to play cards—which indicated that they and we did not think too much of the restriction.

I can't recall attending many lectures and concerts at Bloomington. Of course I.U. did not then have the large world-renowned School of Music and program it now has. Nor would we have had the time to attend very many. We attended at least two concerts, by John McCormack and Martinelli. And of the numerous speakers on the campus I recall at the moment hearing only Carl Sandburg, Harold Laski, and W. E. Hocking, but I know there were others.

The History Club also occupied some of my time and energy, the first year as a member and speaker, the second as president of the club. The group was made up of students interested in history—especially graduate students—and history professors. The first year I was asked to speak on some phase of Abraham Lincoln. Prof. R. C. Buley apparently had suggested this. He and the others must have been satisfied with my performance, for the following year they nominated and elected me as president of the club.

Verna's time was also well occupied, not only as a housekeeper and reading for Mrs. Foster, but with courses at the university. She had taken some graduate work at the University of Iowa in Latin, and at Indiana she took courses in English and English history. One course on the ballad she enjoyed very much was under Prof. Stith Thompson, who was a leading authority in that field. We had some company occasionally, but not enough to add greatly to Verna's housekeeping. We enjoyed having my sister Dot live with us one summer while doing graduate work in English at I.U. A few other relatives came for short visits. When Uncle Ben (Schertz) and Aunt Emma came we showed them some interesting and historic sights in southern Indiana and Kentucky. Indiana is fortunate in having a good system of state parks, some of the most beautiful being in the southern part of the state. Two of these—Brown County and Spring Mill—are close to Bloomington. On one occasion we had some eight or ten guests overnight. In May 1935 the Goshen College seniors took their "sneak" to Spring Mill Park and stopped enroute in Bloomington overnight. The girls in the class—a considerably smaller number than the men—stayed with us and the men slept elsewhere. We were especially pleased to have the group, partly because we had been the faculty sponsors of the class since their freshmen days.

One of the most significant historic sites in southern Indiana is the George Rogers Clark Memorial at Vincennes. In the summer of 1936, I believe it was, Verna and I went to see it dedicated by President Roosevelt. With a sequence of impressive paintings the Memorial illustrates the conquest of the Northwest by Clark in 1778-1779. With such a huge throng of people present, this was not the time to get the best view of the Memorial. We got a better and more leisurely view of it several years later.

Other Goshen people at I.U. added to our enjoyment of the Bloomington years. Among these were Prof. and Mrs. S. W. Witmer, Prof. and Mrs. S. A.

Yoder, and Paton Yoder, one of our history majors. S. W., S. A., and Paton were also working on their Ph.D.s.

My goal was to leave Bloomington in August 1937 and return to Goshen and resume teaching in September. This meant a busy schedule of completing my course work, my language requirements, taking the preliminary doctoral examinations, written and oral, and doing as much research as possible on the dissertation. Since most of the Colfax materials were not at I.U., I of course planned to complete that part of the work later. It took me several days to take the written part of the examinations in my five fields. They were truly "comprehensive" but fair and reasonable. The more tense part was the orals. But I decided to relax and played golf on the morning of the day set for them. One history professor, not on my committee, knew I was to have the exam that afternoon and was surprised to see me playing golf in the morning. He congratulated me and thought it was a good idea. I did too, and it worked. I felt strongly that if five years of graduate work in a well-planned program under good teachers had not adequately prepared me for those exams nothing would have!

CHAPTER 10
Return to Goshen 1937-1943

When we returned to Goshen in September 1937 I would not give teaching my undivided attention because the dissertation was still hanging over my head. The college cooperated in permitting me to teach only twelve hours per week, a bit less than a full load, and allowing me to do my teaching on Mondays, Wednesdays, and Fridays. This left me Tuesdays, Thursdays, and Saturdays for research on the dissertation. Most of this research was done in the library of the Northern Indiana Historical Museum in South Bend, which had quite a few valuable Colfax papers, and virtually a complete file of the South Bend *St. Joseph Valley Register* which Colfax edited, as well as partial but important files of other South Bend papers. *The Register*, at first a weekly and then a daily, was a forerunner of the *South Bend Tribune*, and was clearly very important for a study of Colfax. He was the editor, and even when he was a congressman in Washington he frequently wrote articles for his paper.

In addition to this research I taught an extension course in American history one evening a week in Hammond for Indiana University. The course was a duplicate of one I taught at Goshen, and so it involved no extra preparation. Verna, who assisted me greatly in my research, not only in South Bend but elsewhere, accompanied me those late afternoons on the trips to Hammond.

To complete my research a trip east was necessary, and this was planned for and carried out in the summer of 1938. As usual, Verna accompanied me. Unfortunately the Colfax material has been scattered considerably. But the best source in the East is in the

Library of Congress where a modest collection of Colfax papers is located, along with those of many colleagues with whom he had had correspondence. Other depositories yielding fruitful information were found in Philadelphia, New York City, Providence, at Harvard University in Cambridge, Ithaca, N.Y., Cleveland, and at Hayes Memorial Library in Fremont, Ohio. (For more information on sources, scholars can check the bibliography in my *Schuyler Colfax*, pp.449 ff.)

The "last roundup" or "final hurrah" for the Ph.D. was held at Bloomington in April, 1939. This oral examination, I had been told, was to cover only the dissertation and the field of the dissertation. Professor Lynch surprised me by asking some questions, especially bibliographical, on the French Revolution! I don't think my performance on that point was too dazzlingly brilliant, but I came through all right and got the committee's blessing. I remember, and have tried to follow, Professor Moffat's parting admonition: "Now don't die at the top."

I did not hold Professor Lynch's surprise question against him. We were good friends. Not many days after the examination I went to Memphis, Tennessee, to attend the annual meeting of the Mississippi Valley Historical Association, and to hear Professor Lynch give the presidential address on "The Mississippi Valley and Its History."

By way of further celebration of the completion of the doctorate, we decided to take a trip by car to California in August 1939. I had the courage and took the risk to travel with five women! In addition to Verna, three of her sisters—Anna, Lena, and Esther Graber—and my sister Dorothy traveled with us. Esther, a good typist, had typed my dissertation as my Ph.D. gift, and so I refused any contribution from her for transportation expenses.

We followed fairly closely the route which Colfax took in 1865 when he traveled with a small group to Atchison, Kansas, by train, and from there westward by stagecoach to Denver, Salt Lake City, Virginia City, Nevada, and San Francisco. After picking up Anna at Rock Falls, Illinois, we traveled to Omaha and Ft. Kearney, Nebraska, where we joined the route that the Colfax party had taken in 1865. In a restaurant at Julesburg, Colorado, we were surprised to have waiters serve us who, attracted by the Goshen College sweaters some of our group were wearing, informed us that they knew and were related to Sanford C. Yoder, president of Goshen College. Julesburg was only a few miles from Chappell, Nebraska, where Sanford once lived. In Denver and surrounding area we spent several days visiting the historic and scenic sights before going on to Salt Lake City by way of Laramie, Wyoming.

I have always felt especially fortunate about one visit we made in Denver on this trip. This was a visit to Mrs. Frank Hall, widowed wife of the secretary of the Territory of Colorado. In her nineties in 1939, she was very close to the Colfax family, and made the journey with them to Colorado in 1868. Because of her many years in that state, she was able to tell us interesting stories of the West, as well as fill in some details about Colfax. One of these stories had to do with her attending the ceremonies held in connection with the completion of the transcontinental railroad at Promontory, Utah, in 1869.

Salt Lake City, which we were seeing for the first time, impressed me a great deal. You could almost feel history striking you in the face. Seldom has a people used history to promote their cause as the Mormons have. The organ recital in the Tabernacle, especially the playing of "Come, Come Ye Saints," was an unforgettable experience. The printed programs that the ushers at the entrances handed out contained the words and a brief history of this famous song. Since I was the lone man with five women in our car, I was a man of some stature in this city of the saints. While parked at the temple square a guide came by and tried to sell us some tours in the city. While telling us the story of Brigham Young and his wives, the guide took a further look at the occupants of our car and exclaimed to me: "Say, you didn't do so badly yourself, did you?" I explained that all the women were related to me. "I suppose they are," shot back the guide—as much as to say that Brigham Young was related to all his wives too!

From Salt Lake City we proceeded westward to Virginia City by way of Ely and Austin. Just before reaching Ely we had our first flat tire. I explained and demonstrated to the girls my philosophy of changing tires: first relax, rest and meditate for awhile in order to get properly oriented before taking the next step. The girls however didn't quite understand my profound philosophy on this point and got out and started changing the tire themselves. This fact did not disturb my equilibrium too much; but when several men came along, stopped, and started helping the girls my manhood and spirit of service were aroused to the point where I could not resist the impulse to assist the ladies. With such a spirit of unanimity, where *all* were (finally) minded to work, we soon had the job accomplished, we thanked the men for their gallantry, and were on our way. It was dark when we reached Ely. This was unfortunate, for the motel selected by Dot and Anna that night was probably the lousiest of the trip. But we got through the night, and had many laughs about Ely ever since.

Like the Colfax party in 1865, we too had to stop at historic Virginia City. It was in this famous mining city that Colfax delivered his longest speech on mining, about which he had talked with President Lincoln on the night before his assassination. Colfax had given a shorter version of the address in Central City, Colorado. Home of the famous Comstock Lode, Virginia City had by 1939 long since become a ghost town, but enough important remnants of its historic past, including Mark Twain's writing and publishing interests, remained to make it still attractive for tourists and historians.

From Virginia City we proceeded to beautiful Lake Tahoe where we spent the night in lovely log cabins, enjoying the cool embracing air of that area. The next morning we drove to the famous Donner Pass, Donner Lake, and the nearby Donner Memorial. Here occurred in the fall and winter of 1846-47 one of the worst tragedies in the history of the western migrations. Enroute to California, the Donner Party from Illinois took a new ill-advised route south of Great Salt Lake rather than the old one by way of Ft. Hall. Because of difficulties in crossing the Wahsatch Mountains and longer-than-expected deserts, they arrived late in the Sierra Nevada Mountains. The snow, coming earlier than usual, trapped the party in the mountains just a bit short of the pass. The tragedy brought out the best and the worst in man. The snow became so deep—twenty-two feet at the monument—that relief parties also became engulfed in the snow, lost some of their members, and a few had to turn back in failure. The party in the mountains suffered indescribable hardships. Some ate the flesh of dead bodies to survive. A few refused. The relief parties that got through saved forty-seven of the eighty-seven caught in the mountains. Apparently the last to perish was George Donner's wife, Tamsen, the pathos and poignancy of whose death can scarcely be equated in life or fiction. When the third relief party came in late March 1847, she was faced with the difficult ethical question of leaving her dying husband, who was too ill to leave, and go with the relief party and her children to rear them in California—as Donner urged—or remain with him the few hours or days he still had to live, and then face death herself. Having been assured that friends would help with the children, and reared with such standards of conjugal fidelity that she could not face the future were she to leave her dying husband, Tamsen Donner decided to remain. To this day Californians acclaim Tamsen Donner as one of the great heroines of the state. Incidentally we met some of the Donner descendants at the unveiling of "This is the Place Monument" near Salt Lake City in July, 1947.

Leaving this presently pleasant scene—whose history concealed such dreadful horrors—we drove down from Donner Pass via Placerville (Hangtown) to Sutter's Fort, where we stopped for a short visit, and then on to San Francisco. After visiting the chief historic sites and the San Francisco World's Fair, we journeyed to Yosemite and then to Los Angeles, stopping there a few days for a visit with Uncle Jake Conrads and the tourist attractions in the area.

On the return trip from Los Angeles we made stops at Grand Canyon, La Junta, Colorado, and Hesston, Kansas. As we left the orange country in California we encountered a roadside orange juice market with this sign: "All the orange juice you can drink for 10 cents." I was looking for such a place, and what a wonderful way of leaving the state full of pleasant memories, I thought. So I loaded up with California (Sunkist) sunshine! I paid for my folly a day or two later. Yes, I had "memories" of California, but they were not so pleasant! On the bleak desert of New Mexico restrooms and even bridges—under which one could retreat with some privacy—were far too scarce for comfort for one in my deplorable condition! Finally we did cross a bridge. I stopped the car and "ran for cover." Did the female passengers sympathize with me? Hardly! My sister even took a picture of me running for refuge!

In the meantime we stopped to see the magnificent Grand Canyon. But the girls, like so many of their sex, took a brief glimpse of the "huge gully" and then spent most of their time in the souvenir shop buying and sending home postcards showing the awe-inspiring scenes they were enjoying!

We of course stopped at La Junta where some of us had lived and where all of us had many friends. Anna had taken her nurses training here and had taught for a short period. Our friends had arranged a picnic supper for us in the city park, and we thus got to see many more of them in the short visit than we otherwise would have.

Stopping at Hesston for a short visit was also a must. Three of us had attended school here, and of course the S. B. King relatives were there. One night Alvin royally entertained us with an excellent meal at the Harvey House in Newton. But the weather was so hot that, as I recall, instead of remaining over a second night, we started out toward midnight for Sterling, Illinois, where we remained with Anna during the following night before going on to Goshen the next day.

It was a short trip, but we had seen much, and all, I think, found it an interesting and profitable three weeks spent together. This was the only trip which Anna shared with us and one of the few to the West in which Art did not participate.

More travel was "just around the corner," but in the meantime there was teaching to do. I found the combination of study, teaching, and travel stimulating and challenging—the more so as I became more experienced in each of these areas. One of course learns much as one teaches. But the more knowledge of the subject that the teacher brings to the classroom, the more confidence and enthusiasm he has, and the more stimulating he becomes as an instructor in history. And the more that one can present material from the angle of "having been there," of having observed firsthand "on location," the more one can make what too many think is a dead subject come alive.

I was grateful for the fact that my doctoral studies required five fields—in my case modern European history, government, and economics, in addition to my two fields in U.S. history—rather than just one narrow field in history. These cognate studies complemented and fortified my main field, U.S. history, thus making me a more able teacher in that area. For a few years I taught a few economics courses. I was glad to be relieved of that when Carl Kreider joined the faculty. For many more years I taught American government. This was so close to U.S. history, especially constitutional history, that I was glad to do it and felt that the knowledge of it greatly aided in teaching my chief field. The same was true of recent European history. Because of having studied under F. Lee Benns at I.U., Professor Hershberger wanted me to teach that course, which I did for a few years.

One of my faculty committee assignments during these years and for many more to come, was to serve as chairman of the Lecture-Music Committee. This really required much time and effort. My basic philosophy was that if we would put on a good program, and let the public know about it, they would support it, and thus the general public and the college community would benefit, for the latter alone would not bear the expense burden for the quality program I had in mind. I always had a good committee that supported that kind of program. I shall say more in a later chapter about the outstanding numbers we had after we had larger auditoriums in which to hold the L-M Series.

In 1940 and 1941 it was time to do more traveling. In the summer of 1940 Art, Dot, Verna and I followed the Abraham Lincoln trail from his birthplace near Hodgenville, Kentucky, to his boyhood home in southern Indiana, and then on to near Decatur, Illinois, and then to New Salem and Springfield. (In our case, to save mileage we saw Springfield first and then New Salem.) We had hoped that Uncle C. Henry Smith, who was much interested in Lincoln, would be one of our party. He had intended at first to accompany us, but because of Aunt Laura not feeling well he had to change his plans.

I have always been intrigued by the phenominal career of Abraham Lincoln—not only because he came from Illinois and practiced law in Metamora, one of my home towns—but because of his achievements in view of his background. Professor Edward Channing has summed it up well: "The career of Abraham Lincoln casts a doubt on all our ideas of heredity and education. Elaborate genealogical studies . . . have . . . failed to disclose any ancestor . . . who possessed anything approaching the qualities of mind and command of Abraham Lincoln. As to education, he had nothing that a pedagogical professor of the present day would recognize by that word." Hence our interest in looking more closely at part of the environment of this remarkable person, of whom at his death E. M. Stanton could properly say: "Now he belongs to the ages."

Another valuable trip we made a bit later was our first venture into Mexico. Our Christmas vacation during the winter of 1940-1941, a bit longer than usual, was used for this occasion. Art Smith, Lois Gunden, French teacher at Goshen College, my brother Tilman, then head of the high school at Roanoke, Illinois, and

Verna and I made up the party. We traveled to Mexico City over the new Panamerican Highway, crossing the border at Laredo, Texas. This all-paved highway, recently completed, opened up some places that had been so isolated that no automobiles were to be found there until the construction of the road.

Indeed the concept of the typical American was that Mexico was not only isolated but also a dangerous area in which to travel. This was a hangover from the days of the Revolution when Pancho Villa and other revolutionaries were a little rough on Americans. This fear is illustrated by the story of an American businessman in the 1930s who needed to travel to Mexico for business purposes. He first sent a telegram to our ambassador Josephus Daniels in Mexico City, asking whether it was safe for him to come to Mexico. Daniels, according to the story, immediately telegraphed him: ''Perfectly safe if you don't come by way of Chicago!'' But Mexico has been a victim of penetration and exploitation (particularly by Americans), especially under Porfirio Diaz, who was finally overthrown in the Revolution of 1910-1911. There were reasons for the Revolution. Under Diaz, as someone aptly stated, Mexico had become the ''mother of aliens and the stepmother of Mexicans.'' So the efforts of Mexicans since 1910-1911 have been justifiably aimed at again becoming householders in their own household. But those traveling in Mexico in 1940 were as safe as those traveling in the U.S.

Upon the recommendation of our friend and teaching colleague, Noble Kreider, we stayed at Hotel Ontario. We hired a guide for the first day or two and then proceeded on our own. During the six or seven days we had for the city and its environs, we saw the following among others: the Zocalo, Cathedral, National Museum (which contained the famous Aztec

Calendar), National Palace (with its famous murals painted by Diego Rivera), oldest hospital in western hemisphere, built by Cortes with church attached, Palace of Fine Arts, Chapultepec Castle, Tree of the Sad Night (under which, it is said, Cortes wept after his defeat in 1520), Church of the Virgin Guadalupe, Floating Gardens, a bull fight, pyramids of the Sun and Moon, Cuernavaca, and Taxco. We also saw the University of Mexico, then still in scattered buildings in downtown Mexico City. In one of these buildings we were impressed with a painting entitled "American Imperialism." It portrayed a Mexican lying on the ground with an American standing over him and bayoneting him.

Unfortunately I came into Mexico City with a cold which I had caught enroute the day before. So I remained in bed the first day and became acquainted, of all things, with Alka-Seltzer. Produced in Elkhart, ten miles from my home, I had to go to Mexico City to have my first pill! Those in charge at the hotel sang its praises as a cold remedy, and when Verna went to the drug store the pharmacist also recommended it. So Alka-Seltzer it was! The remedy, plus the rest in bed, worked pretty well. I was out on a limited basis the next day. One plus came partly by accident. During the day I was ill, our group, while talking with a guard at the National or Presidential Palace, asked him whether it would be possible to talk with the recently inaugurated President Camacho. The guard said he thought it possible and told our group to come back at a certain time the next noon. When we came at the appointed time, the presidential aide came out and told us the president could not see us then but we should return that evening. We did that and went into a large waiting room filled with people, all waiting to see the president. I had visions of having to wait for hours to see the executive, if at all, and in view of my cold, though much improved, I thought I had better retire to my hotel and go to bed. Later that evening Verna and the others came to my room and surprised me by saying they conferred with the president shortly after I had left! They reported having had a very pleasant visit. Possibly one thing that helped them get in as soon as they did was the fact that another American tourist, knowledgeable in building railroads, happened to be in our group, and the aide might have reported this to Camacho who was much interested in that subject.

The historic sites mentioned above were all clearly worth visiting. The Floating Gardens, which have not floated for centuries, probably came closest to being overblown. But with their flowers, decorated boats, and masses of people, they present a show that every visitor will want to see at least once or twice.

The bull fights also are worth seeing once or twice if one is interested in studying Mexican history and culture as I was. But I am glad we do not have bull fights in the U.S. Mexicans defended them, however, as a fine art—a contest between the superior mind of physically weaker men and brute force as represented by the bull. But on the day we attended, the fight did not quite measure up to the above standard. For brute force won over the mind of man—an exception to the rule. We saw the greatest bull fighter in Mexico, Alberto Balderas, meet an untimely death on his thirtieth birthday. Somehow or other, he made a misstep and the bull gored him. Balderas got up, was helped to the infirmary, and only later—but before we left the ring—did we hear that he had died. The irony of it was that he had earlier given a spectacular performance, had easily dispatched his bull, to the bravos of the crowd, and had now voluntarily reentered the ring to help out a fellow-matador who was having trouble killing his bull. The story made the papers not only in Mexico but in the U.S.

After about a week's visit of historic sites and events we returned to the U.S. by the same route, grateful for a richly-rewarding trip to a foreign culture so near us, and also thankful for our own homeland.

The following June (1941) found us further exploring more of our own country. Art, Lena Graber, Verna and I followed the old Santa Fe Trail, as closely as possible, from New Franklin, Missouri, where it originally began, to Santa Fe, New Mexico. (Some years later the starting point was at Independence, Missouri.) It is an interesting coincidence that New Franklin is across the Missouri River from Boonville, Missouri, which city and the county in which it is located were named after the pioneer woodsman, Daniel Boone, who moved to this area from Kentucky in his later years. Kit Carson, a younger pioneer scout and trapper, also came to Missouri by way of Kentucky and lived in this same community. But he was itching to go farther west and did join a Santa Fe expedition to New Mexico. It is said that Daniel Boone, who as a pioneer felt crowded when "someone moved within forty miles of him," had the same itch in his older years and had to be discouraged and almost restrained from doing so.

So New Franklin was an appropriate starting point for the Santa Fe Trail, and it was where we started our trek in 1941. We went on to Independence, later the famous starting point for both the Santa Fe and Oregon Trails. Both trails followed the same route south westward for about forty miles to what is now Gardner, Kansas, where the travelers reached a fork in the road—one leading northwest to Oregon and the other southwest to Santa Fe. There used to be a simple sign here pointing northwest which read, "Road to

Oregon.'' These were three words ''which changed the course of life itself for those who took that turning.'' (Irene Paden, *The Wake of the Prairie Schooner*, 27.) One writer observed that so ''simple a sign never before announced so long a journey.'' I would have given a lot to have seen this old sign. Unfortunately, by 1941 it had long since disappeared. But the ''turning'' meant that those who took it were very probably going for life, whereas those continuing southwest were going as traders and would likely return soon.

From Gardner we followed the trail westward to Council Grove, Kansas, an important point where the Santa Fe traders met to form wagon trains for the seventy-day wagon trek to Santa Fe. U.S. 56 in Kansas follows the old trail fairly closely and this is the route we followed. Shortly before we arrived, there had been heavy rains and flooded roads, some of which were closed. Significantly, U.S. 56 was not one of these. The early travelers had faced this same problem and apparently had learned to pick out the high ground as their route.

At Hillsboro—the trail ran just south of it—we detoured to Hesston for a day or two to visit relatives. Upon resuming the trek, we hunted out the Cooprider farm near McPherson upon which the trail had left marks which could still be seen even after sixty years of farming and plowing.

I have always had a personal interest in Great Bend, Kansas, where the trail met the Arkansas River. Here it was that father, when about sixteen, investigated the possibility of attending a private school there, but discovered the few funds he had saved would be inadequate. He gave up the effort with regret. But the incident indicated to us that father, who had not been able to secure much formal education, supported it and helped his children to obtain it. I thought enough of my dad's interest and effort to take a picture of the building—in 1941 used for other purposes—which served as the educational institution.

From Great Bend the Santa Fe Trail followed the Arkansas River to La Junta, Colorado. As before, we continued to stop at the historic places along the trail. One of these was Dodge City, with its Boot Hill, which secured its fame later as a cow town at the end of the long cattle drives from the South. One elderly person there in particular aroused our attention. In the 1880s, in addition to having been a cowboy, he had served in various local offices such as constable, marshal, justice of the peace, and sheriff. He made the significant remark that in the 1880s one could ride his horse to Dodge City, take off his saddle, and tether him on the edge of the town, and come back in the evening to unfailingly find everything as one had left it in the morning. He then added: "You know you can't do that anymore" — an interesting comment on the wild days of Dodge City!

We also paused briefly at the famous Bent's Fort just east of La Junta. There was nothing left of it except the uneven ground that indicated where the foundation was located. Since 1941 a replica of the old fort has been restored. And of course we had to stop at La Junta—this time very briefly—to say hello to a few old friends.

At La Junta, which means the junction, the trail left the Arkansas River, headed southwest toward Trinidad, and then Raton Pass, Taos, and Santa Fe in New Mexico. I should add that there developed early in the life of the trail the Cimarron cutoff which left the trail near the present Cimarron, Kansas, and headed southwest along the Cimarron valley. This was shorter, but presented more of a water problem than the old route.

My attitude toward ruts on the Santa Fe Trail (or any other) was quite different in 1941 from what it was in 1914 when I first lived at La Junta. Now we did everything we could to find old remnants. In 1914 we did everything we could to avoid them. (Then they were a nuisance because one's car center was too likely to hit the ground and thus get hung up, if indeed it didn't damage the transmission.) And we did find some parts of the old trail where the ruts were clearly visible—some in Kansas, and some southwest of La Junta. I got so absorbed in ruts that some of my friends, including students, thought I had "rutitus."

We of course had to stop at Taos. Taos was already a colorful old Indian town in 1540 when some of Coronado's men discovered it. The Taos Indians have played an important part in the early history of New Mexico, giving the Spanish a rough time when they later came to colonize and to evangelize the Indians. Eventually Taos became a great fur-trading center—attracting Kit Carson and many others—and still later a center for American artists.

In Santa Fe, the objective of our trek, we remained for several days. Santa Fe has always fascinated me, and never more than on this first occasion. At that time it still seemed like an extension of old Mexico, which it was of course for many years. The promenade (*paseo*) at the central plaza—in which the young men would walk in one direction and the *senoritas* in the opposite—was exactly the same as in Mexico. Unfortunately, in later visits to Santa Fe it seemed to us that the city was losing some of its "Spanishness" and becoming too modernized and Anglicized.

But the Santa Fe traders were more interested in commerce than in culture. After Mexico became independent from Spain in 1821, the Santa Fe trade was opened to Americans and became profitable to both sides, the Americans taking manufactured goods, and bringing back wool, mules, and especially, much-needed silver. This trade grew in the following years, and the trail was important—even after New Mexico became a part of U.S. in 1848—until the Santa Fe railroad reached Santa Fe in 1880.

From Santa Fe we journeyed south to Carlsbad Caverns. In my judgment, these caverns are the most beautiful and majestic in U.S. We then proceeded westward to El Paso, Tucson, and Phoenix, enjoying enroute White Sands National Monument and the varieties of cacti and other vegetation of the southwest. Vegetation was more colorful here in this June of 1941 because of more and later rain than usual. One time Uncle C. Henry Smith had offered me some land free near Casa Grande if I would pay the back taxes. Often since then I have been sorry that I did not take him up on his generous offer.

After visiting relatives in the Casa Grande and Phoenix area, we headed north by way of beautiful Oak Creek Canyon for the Grand Canyon country. Being that close to this majestic scene, we felt we had to fill again our cup of inspiration. From here we proceeded to the more delicate beauty of Bryce Canyon, and also Zion National Parks in southern Utah. I call the more delicate, exquisite Bryce Canyon the Mozart of our national parks, and Zion the Brahms, as compared with Grand Canyon—the massive, majestic, monumental Beethoven.

We then explored new territory through scenic Monument Valley and the arches country in souteastern Utah. The lack of good roads made this very scenic land a neglected area. But this has now been remedied. Even with the poorer roads then existing we felt deeply rewarded by our visit to this fairyland left by millenniums of erosion.

Turning eastward through Grand Junction, Glenwood Springs, and Rocky Mountain National Park, we absorbed more of the beauties of colorful Colorado. A state that I detested in 1914, by 1941 Colorado had, as I have often put it, "more beauty per square inch than any other state in the union." Continuing eastward through Kansas, I think it was on this occasion that we stopped at Goodland to visit a Morman cousin of Verna and Lena. It was probably on this trip when we stopped in St. Joseph, Missouri, to visit the headquarters of the Pony Express, which in 1860-1861 contributed a brief but dramatic chapter in the history of our efforts to speed up communication. After eighteen months of operation the Pony Express was put out of business by the completion of the transcontinental telegraph line in October 1861.

From St. Joseph we headed toward Goshen by way of Eureka, Illinois, where we left Art off.

1941 was a year in which world conditions worsened. World War II, which had broken out in 1939, was becoming increasingly complicated for the U.S. The extent to which our own President Roosevelt himself made things more complex for our country need not be gone into at this point. Suffice it to say we were drifting closer and closer to our entrance into the conflict. The Selective Service Act of 1940 and 1941 provided for the drafting of young men, and included provisions for conscientious objectors to serve in Civilian Public Service camps instead of going into the armed forces. The war thus greatly reduced the male student population in our colleges and made it possible for these institutions to operate with smaller faculties.

At the same time (1941) Bethel College at North Newton, Kansas, lost a history teacher, Professor Harshbarger, through illness and death. President Ed Kaufman telephoned me some time after I had returned to Goshen and asked whether I might be able to help them out for a year or two. He had been somewhere in the East and called me on his way home. He wanted to come up and see me. I had told him—because of reduced enrollment—that Professor Guy F. Hershberger could probably take care of the history teaching for the time being. During the course of our telephone conversation President Kaufman found out I was a nephew of C. Henry Smith. Kaufman's response amused me: "Well, if you are a nephew of C. Henry Smith I won't have to come to see you. I am ready to hire you over the telephone." I thanked him for the compliment to my uncle, and said I would seriously consider the matter.

About the same time, however, other developments had occurred that made it necessary for me to remain at Goshen. Guy F. Hershberger accepted a request from the Mennonite Central Committee to serve as educational director in one of the recently established Civilian Public Service camps (C.P.S.). I informed President Kaufman of Bethel that I would now have to remain at Goshen. But I recommended Melvin Gingerich, history teacher in the high school and junior college at Washington, Iowa, as one who might be interested. Kaufman contacted Gingerich, with the result that Melvin and his family moved to Bethel where he taught for a much longer period than I would have been able to do. I was happy that this mutually satisfactory arrangement worked out so well.

CHAPTER 11
"Paraguayan Interlude"
1944-1945

It appears that this chapter will be the most difficult one to write—not because of a shortage of material, but because there is too much. We have written a book of some 180 pages on the subject (*Paraguayan Interlude: Observation and Impressions*, Herald Press, 1950). Hence the use of quotes in the title of this chapter. Unfortunately, the book has been out of print for nearly thirty years, though it can be found in many libraries. So I suppose the best thing to do is to compromise and put the highlights of this experience in this work.

The urge to do some kind of relief work or service for my church and/or country remained with me since World War I. I have always had an immense appreciation for the freedom and liberty—including religious—that we Americans have enjoyed in this great land of ours. I say this despite my awareness of gaps and inadequacies in some cases such as our treatment of the Indians and Blacks. Especially in respecting the freedom of religious conscience the great majority of Americans, as represented through our government, have gone out of their way to be sensitive on this point—a record which only those who share our English political and constitutional traditions can match. In World War I, I was a bit too young to be drafted and in World War II, I was a little too old. In about 1920 Joe Graber and I, while students at Hesston College, offered our services to Mennonite Central Committee (MCC) for doing relief work in Europe or the Near East. But we were turned down on the grounds of being too young.

So in World War II the question of obligation arose again, and Verna shared my convictions. In 1943 I first offered my services to the U.S. Government, which had shortly before sent out a request to college professors to fill temporary jobs in the foreign service, including Latin American countries. I had thought of serving in some country like Argentina, Chile, or Peru where the climate was decent, but not in hot Paraguay. An F.B.I. agent came to Goshen to check me out. All went well, and he then asked for a conference with me at a certain hour later in the day. Something went amiss, however, just before the conference. The F.B.I. agent had found out somehow or other that twenty years earlier I had been hospitalized a year or so for illness, and he called off the conference. So MCC sent me to Paraguay for service, to which I probably would not have gone for the U.S. Government. However, the hot summers were bearable, and the other seasons, save for an occasional dust storm in winter, were agreeable.

The reason for our going to Paraguay was the presence of about 5,000 Mennonites, with more coming after World War II. MCC felt responsible especially for some 2,000 Mennonite refugees who were able to leave Russia in the late 1920s and early 1930s, and who had come to Paraguay at the suggestion and with the help of MCC. At that particular time Paraguay was virtually the only country that opened its doors to these refugees from Russia on the basis of full religious liberty, and with no discrimination against the many who were suffering from trachoma. The religious liberty included exemption from military service. The Russian Mennonites settled in the Chaco—that part of Paraguay west of the Paraguay River—where the Canadian Mennonites had settled a few years before.

When we went to Paraguay in January 1944 MCC was enlarging its work in that country and was recruiting a larger work force for service there. Dr.

John Schmidt and his wife Clara, a registered nurse, were already in Fernheim (the Russian Mennonite colony) engaged in health work. This included administering a hospital and training practical nurses. Vernon Schmidt had recently come to help the colony build roads, among other things, and Dr. G. S. Klassen had recently arrived to provide much-needed dental service. One thing he did in addition was to train several young Mennonites to continue dental work after he left. Mrs. Klassen, a home economist, put her talents to good use in teaching Mennonite women better use of their available resources for cooking. Robert Geigly had come to Asuncion in 1943, accompanied for a very short period by A. E. Janzen. Geigley's assignment was to search for a house in the capitol that could serve as a center for Mennonites, including that of a low-priced hostelry for those coming to the city on business, and to think and plan for some kind of service to the Paraguayans as a thank-you project for their generous acceptance of the Mennonite immigrants. So the enlargement of old projects, plus the new ones mentioned above, together with others still to come—such as helping with their schools, surveying of land, building telephone lines—required more personnel and administrative organization. I was asked to serve as Director of MCC work in Paraguay, and Verna was to serve as matron of the new Mennonite Home in Asuncion.

Our work was largely confined to the Russian Mennonites, but later the Canadian Mennonites also developed closer relations with MCC and received some aid. These Canadians were from among the most conservative in western Canada, although not quite so conservative as the Old Colony Mennonites who had gone to Mexico in the earlier 1920s. They were better off economically than the Russian Mennonites, and they did not have as much dissension among them over Nazi politics as did the group from Russia. This dissension was serious by 1944, and part of our work as an MCC was to help heal this schism.

Our journey to Paraguay, beginning early in January, was a long one. We first went to Akron, Pennsylvania, MCC headquarters, for orientation, and then—after returning to Goshen—to New Orleans to board the Argentine ship, Rio Jachal, for Buenos Aires. The route was a bit circuitous and took about four weeks. Unfortunately, some of our important baggage did not get on the Rio Jachal in New Orleans. Our experienced missionary friends in Argentina urged us to wait for the baggage and claim it personally if we wanted to be sure of getting it. This meant a wait of about three weeks. The time was not wasted, however. We spent it visiting some of our missions in Argentina, and I took a course at the Berlitz School to improve my German. It was at this point also that Sarah Histand, an MCC worker from Pennsylvania who came with us, was married to Vernon Schmidt in the Bragado Mennonite Church, missionaries T. K. Hershey, Amos Swartzentruber, and Nelson Litwiller officiating. Vernon and Sarah had asked me to play the part of her father in giving away the bride. I said I would be glad to do so but warned them I had never done it before. Vernon's encouraging response was: "Well, all you have to do is turn her loose." So all of us played our parts without mishap, and it was a happy occasion. Vernon and Sarah accompanied us on the delightful river trip to Asuncion in March 1944.

When we arrived in Asuncion, Robert Geigley—who had been in Bueno Aires a short time but had returned ahead of us—and Kornelius Walde, a young Mennonite in the capital city, met us at the port and helped us through customs. Due to the smallness of the house then serving for a short time as a Mennonite Center, we stayed in Hotel Argentina until we found a more adequate Mennonite home.

We soon found the problems awaiting us greater and more complex than we had anticipated. Reports were emanating from the Chaco that some kind of a "revolution" had occurred in Fernheim whereby the old colony administration was turned out and a new one voted in. The old one had been more pro-Nazi in its political orientation, but the lines were blurred somewhat, and other more personal issues were also involved. In any case Nazi politics were a disturbing factor even in this faraway, allegedly isolated Chaco. The United States and her allies had drawn up a blacklist of German or pro-German business concerns with which we Americans were not supposed to deal. Almost as soon as I arrived in Asuncion, the U.S. embassy officials called me over to apprise me of the serious political situation that had arisen in Fernheim and were about to put the whole colony on the blacklist, which would have made it impossible for us as an MCC or as Americans to work at all with the Mennonites. I explained that I had just arrived, that I was going to Fernheim in a few days to see what happened, and asked them to delay any action until I returned and reported. This the embassy officials were glad to do.

Verna accompanied me on my first trip to the Chaco. We took the usual route at that time: river boat to Puerto Casado, narrow gauge railway from there to "Kilometer 145," and by spring wagon from there. The first stage was a distance of some 300 miles, and the last about seventy miles to Filadelfia. We had to wait two days in Puerta Casado for the train, but the time was not wasted. I got acquainted with the industry of the port, and talked with people, especially Jose Casado—an Argentine who was in immediate charge of his family's huge land and cattle interests in the Chaco—and his administrator, a Mr. McLean. These gentlemen also indicated how serious it would have been if Fernheim had been put on the blacklist.

For years I had been hearing, reading, and teaching about the *Gran Chaco*. And now at last we were to see for ourselves what it was like! Two coaches at the rear of the freight train supplied "luxurious" accommodations for a motley crowd of passengers—soldiers, Casado employees, Mennonites, and others. In both coaches the seats were upholstered with comfortable (?) wooden slats. But the trip was not too unpleasant except for mosquitoes. The train didn't travel rapidly enough to keep ahead of them. The mosquitoes did not become "serious" until about four o'clock in the afternoon. With their hands and feet flying in every direction, the passengers engaged in such a furious onslaught against these pests that it was dangerous to remain seated or to walk in the aisle. But by six-thirty or seven p.m. we arrived at "Kilometer 145" with no one fatally injured.

At this end-station the scene was a busy one. Quite a few Mennonites were there eating supper around their camp fires, having brought cotton or other products to be shipped to Asuncion. Some of the animals used were oxen instead of horses, another factor reminding one of frontier days in U.S. a century earlier. Franz Wiens of Fernheim had come to take us in his spring wagon on the seventy-mile journey to Filadelfia. After eating a lunch prepared by him we drove off into the Chaco night. Meeting a number of Mennonites bringing cotton to the end-station, we drove until about three a.m. and then put up for "the night"—which meant until about six o'clock—in an old shack. After a breakfast of coffee, eggs, *zweibach* (bread) and tangerines, we arrived at our destination in Filadelfia about noon.

136

So at long last we had reached the object of our long journey—Filadelfia (Philadelphia), the city of brotherly love, which was not so "brotherly" in recent weeks and months. The first thing we did of course was to meet with the MCC workers, who were there during the "revolution," to get their picture of what happened. We then visited many others, both leaders and non-leaders on both sides of the controversy. As time went on we began to gain a pretty clear picture—at least a much clearer picture—of the serious misunderstandings that had arisen. I visited also the leaders of nearby Menno colony. Thus we were soon able to make progress in helping Fernheim with her school problems, in road building and communication, reduction of debts owed the Casado company, the medical work, and others.

Religiously, the Fernheim Mennonites were divided into three groups or divisions that had already occurred in Russia: groups in North America corresponding to the General Conference Mennonites, the Mennonite Brethren, and the Evangelical Mennonite Brethren. But they worked together much more closely in Paraguay than here. Unfortunately, the Mennonite Brethren in Fernheim were so divided in their attitude towards Nazi politics that in 1944 they split into two groups over the question. Fortunately, they were reunited in 1947.

All of the five or six trips—by boat, train, autovia, and airplane—I made to the Chaco during the course of our stay of nearly two years had their interesting, not to say, exciting moments. "But for interest and adventure, the first trip, long and wearisome though it was, stands out in memory above them all."

The trip back to Asuncion was by the same route. Annie Enss, a young Mennonite girl from Fernheim, returned with us to work for us in the *Mennoniten Heim*

(Mennonite Home) that we were about to establish. Back in Asuncion the first thing I did was, as promised, to report to the U.S. Embassy what I found in the Chaco. The officials seemed pleased with the report and that new and more cooperative officers were in control of colony affairs. The embassy officials of course did not go ahead with their plan to put Fernheim—actually the Fernheim cooperative—on the blacklist. The next item of business was to find a new house in Asuncion to serve as a Mennonite Center or Home, large enough to house the MCC workers in the city, the hired girls, the four nurses in training in the city, and the Mennonites from the colony who came for business and other purposes and wanted low-cost meals and lodging. We were fortunate in finding a place on Calle Eligio Ayala near the one started the year before. Kornelius Walde, a young Mennonite businessman who frequently assisted us, also roomed in the home. But the demand for rooms grew beyond our expectations, and in a few months we took advantage of the opportunity to rent a still larger house next door and operated the two of them as a unit. The two together were adequate for some time, beyond our period of service.

In July 1944 Orie O. Miller, MCC secretary-treasurer, came to Paraguay on a commissioner trip to discuss with the MCC workers and colony leaders the enlarging program, and also to assess the recent events, especially the new developments—which I had been reporting—in Fernheim. Since time was of the essence for Orie, we arranged to take him to the Chaco and back by airplane. It so happened that members of the U.S. Air Mission to Paraguay wanted to see the Mennonite colonies and the Chaco where they lived. They were delighted to arrange to take us out and back without cost to us. At that time there was no airport in the colonies, and so we landed in a peanut field. The landing of a plane in a community where none had ever landed naturally caused a great deal of excitement. Within minutes scores of people came to see what had happened. Our leaving three days later was a gala occasion for the hundreds, including many children dismissed from school, who had come to see us take off. Landing in a peanut field was one thing. Taking off was another. The ground was too soft for the plane to gain altitude as rapidly as necessary. We hit the top of a fence, and a grove of trees loomed up before us. The pilot brought the plane down rather than risk hitting the trees. There was one old rickety truck in the colony. Fortunately it was available to take the passengers— four or five of us—and baggage to an airport at a military post about sixty miles farther west. With the lighter load the pilots were able to take off, and then pick us up at the military post. The damage to the plane was not so great that we could not return to Asuncion. One of our passengers was another girl from Fernheim who was added to our work force in the Mennonite Center. Since Orie was well known and respected by the Mennonite colonists, his explanation in a public meeting of the work of MCC and its attitude toward Nazi politics helped clear the air.

It was also on the occasion of Orie's visit that I made my first visit to Friesland, a Mennonite colony in East Paraguay, and to Primavera, the Hutterite community nearby. Since the Hutterites had a short landing field in their pasture, we hired a small plane which made the trip in about an hour. Friesland was started in 1937 by a group who was dissatisfied with conditions in Fernheim. They came without MCC's encouragement, and so the organization's feeling of responsibility was never so great as it was toward Fernheim. At the same time MCC wanted to encourage these Mennonites as brethren and to help in a more limited way.

At Primavera nearby were the Hutterites, or Society of Brothers. This particular group was founded in 1920 in Germany by Eberhard Arnold, increased in numbers after moving to England, and then, because of war conditions, moved to Paraguay in 1941. MCC helped in this latter move, and also, with the Church of the Brethren and Quakers, helped them build a hospital which was supposed to be available to Mennonites and Paraguayans as well as Hutterites. Hence an interest in visiting Primavera.

Back in Asuncion Orie had time to meet leisurely with us at our new headquarters and discuss the expansion of the work, especially as it applied to the city. He also met other Mennonites in the city who desired to come to the center and meet him. This included those using the Center as a hostelry.

One part of our new work, which Orie of course encouraged, was to start church services for the Mennonites in Asuncion—both for those living there and for those from the colonies who were there over Sundays. For these services we brought in ministers from Fernheim and Friesland, and kept them there at least over two weekends. This gave them an opportunity to visit in Mennonite homes during the week. The General Conference Mennonites in the U.S. supplied some funds for this ministry. In bringing in colony ministers—none were living in Asuncion at that time—we followed a policy of no discrimination against any branch or faction. Likewise at the Center we opened our doors to all factions—all were welcome to use our facilities. This impressed the various groups and there is clear evidence that our policy changed the attitude of some doubting Thomases about the work of the MCC and also that the policy helped reduce the strained relations between the factions.

At first we held the church services in the Center. But when this facility shortly became too small, we rented a Baptist church a few blocks away. We had our worship Sunday afternoons, and after the services invited the attendants to the Home for a light lunch and visiting. Many took advantage of these opportunites and "a good time was had by all." On other weekday evenings also, provision was made for social and religious gatherings, especially for the young people.

When Robert Geigley returned to the U.S. early in 1945 Betty Keeney of Pennsylvania came to administer the so-called thank you project in Itacurubi, a Paraguayan village near Friesland. This consisted of a supplemental school-feeding program and also teaching of school children and their parents how to have a better balanced diet. Tied in with this was a hookworm control project which however did not get under way until 1946.

Other additions to the MCC staff in Asuncion were Mr. and Mrs. Elvin Souder of Pennsylvania, with their baby Jane. Elvin served as treasurer, bookkeeper, and typist, and also assisted me administratively in various ways. Elvin's wife Patty was a registered nurse. Her nursing skill was useful, and she ably assisted Verna in housekeeping.

Also in 1945 Orval Myers, a Purdue engineering graduate, came to survey and build telephone lines in Fernheim, and Waldo and Rachel Hiebert arrived to teach in the Fernheim high school.

Another assignment I carried out in 1945 was a trip to the Mennonites in Brazil. These came from Russia about the same time as those who came to Paraguay. They however had had virtually no contact with each other since. MCC thought it would be good if I could arrange to take a minister or two along and have a fraternal visit. The Fernheim colony officials favored the idea and offered to help pay the expenses if I would take two ministers along. This I was happy to do. Gerhard Giesbrecht, the leader of the Mennonite Brethren, and Jakob Isaak, leader of the General Conference group, accompanied me. The Brazilian Mennonites appreciated this contact with us, and the journey was highly successful. We visited the Mennonites in or near Curitiba in the state of Parana and those farther south in the state of Santa Catharina. This was the original settlement. But economically life was difficult here. Much of the farmland was hilly, some of it so much so—according to a story said to be true—that one farmer fell out of his corn field and had to be hospitalized for his injuries! So the Mennonites began to move to Curitiba and elsewhere in southern Brazil.

While Giesbrecht and Isaak returned directly to Curitiba, I stopped off at Brusque to visit Mrs. Elizabeth Binkele Buettner, who had been a student and matron at Goshen College. She had married a Brazilian German, owner of a textile mill in Brusque, and was now living here as a widow with her two children. Elizabeth insisted I remain an extra day and then return to Curitiba by car with one of her company's employees. This is the only time in my life that I traveled in an automobile that used gas made from burning charcoal rather than the regular gasoline. Instead of driving up to a gas station and filling up with gasoline we drove up to a coal station and filled up with charcoal! Because of the gas shortage then, one saw many cars with these charcoal-burning attachments on the rear.

While arranging in Curitiba for the return trip to Paraguay, it turned out that space on the next plane was available for two but not three. So I insisted that Giesbrecht and Isaak, who were anxious to return to

142

their families in the Chaco, use the space. I waited two days longer for the next plane. Enroute to Asuncion I stopped at Iguassu Falls to visit one of the greatest scenic wonders of the world. Higher and wider than Niagara, with a greater variety of falls and formations, Iguassu, in my judgment, has the edge on all-around beauty. I was sorry that Verna was not there to share this majestic scene with me. Fortunately, she saw it when we visited South America in 1965.

All three of us who visited the Brazilian brethren felt that the trip was very much worthwhile, a view shared by those in Brazil who kept insisting that our visit was too short. This appreciation was indicated not only to us personally. A leader of the Curitiba Mennonites said the same thing in a letter he wrote to the editor of the *Menno-Blatt*, a paper published in Fernheim. This letter indicates also the importance of the German language to the Mennonites. Before our arrival in Brazil they had heard that "Herr Smith" would have to speak through an interpreter. The letter then states how pleased they were when "Herr Smith" stepped forward and in good (*verstaendlich*) German, "though with an English accent," gave his message. "When he ended, we said: 'That is not Mr. Smith, but Brother Smith.' " The closest affinity, however, was felt and expressed for Giesbrecht and Isaak who addressed them in "Low German." The writer of the letter continued: "We had to say to ourselves, 'these are not our brothers; they are ourselves, bone of our bone, and flesh of our flesh.' " Though this most-favored position in the inside circle was denied me, because my speech betrayed me, I nevertheless felt a warm hospitality and fellowship with the brethren in Brazil.

I should explain that at that time Brazil prohibited the use of German, which the Mennonites used in their church services, but did permit Low German. Since I did not speak Low German, the brethren thought it would be safe for me as a North American to use the German.

Once back in Asuncion there was still plenty of work to do for the remaining months of our service period. My concern about not being able to complete all the tasks assigned me increased when, soon after returning from Brazil, I became ill with typhoid fever—actually paratyphoid B according to the doctor. The prescription was three weeks in bed and a liquid diet. So for about four weeks I was able to do very little. This meant more work for others, especially for Elvin Souder, my able assistant, and for Verna. Unfortunately, I had not fully recovered when Dr. Henry A. Fast, vice-president of MCC, made a commissioner trip to Paraguay in August, 1945. Elvin accompanied him to Friesland and Itacurubi, and Dr. Schmidt showed him around in Fernheim.

One of our concerns in the closing months of service was a thank-you project in addition to Betty Keeney's supplemental school-feeding program at Itacurubi. One of Paraguay's larger medical problems was taking care of its lepers. Since facilities for taking care of them were quite inadequate, MCC had been discussing for some time the possibility of aid in this area. The Paraguayan government and others encouraged us to proceed. One of the possible sites we considered for such a work was near Concepcion, on the Paraguay River between Asuncion and Puerto Casado. Since my doctor thought I was strong enough to make the easy river journey to Concepcion, Dr. Fast and I, accompanied by Rev. Malcolm Norment of Colegio Internacional, made this trip of investigation.

But working on this leper project was a good example of how necessary it is for North Americans to understand the meaning of those typically Latin

American words: *paciencia* (patience) and *manana* (tomorrow). Various negotiating problems arose, even before the changes in the ministry of health, and later the change in government through revolution delayed the initiating of this badly needed project for several years.

In October 1945 I made another and final trip to the Chaco, with Verna accompanying me as she did on the first. We used the same route and method of transportation, except that we used the autovia (an autombile equipped to run on the railroad track) from Puerto Casado to Kilometer 145 instead of the train. With the Fernheim leaders we planned further for the constructing of the telephone lines, operating an experimental farm, continued aid in the educational program, and the medical work, among others. Dr. A. M. Lohrentz of McPherson, Kansas, ably assisted in 1945 as eye, ear, nose, and throat specialist—der *"KopfDoktor"*, the Mennonites called him. We also discussed the desirablility and possibility of constructing an airport near Filadelfia. Usually, these projects too—like the leper work—required patience. Especially was this true of the telephone line construction, because of shortages of materials during the war.

Visiting and saying good-bye were also part of our interest on this last journey. They had also the usual farewell (*Abschied*) program that they gave MCC workers when finishing their assignments. In my talk to them as my part of the program I tried to be helpful and constructive, and encouraged them to continue on the road toward unity, in which we had observed progress since our first trip to the Chaco. I tried to encourage them also in the faith of which they were a part. "What a tragedy it would be," I said, "if, after 400 years of Mennonite history and after having established so many Fernheims (far-away homes) for conscience sake, you and I should give up the faith for which our fathers suffered and even died. God forbid that we should do this." Regardless of faction, many came to say "Auf Widersehen," and to thank us for our service among them. As we returned to Asuncion, we felt happy about our relationship with our Paraguayan brothers and sisters.

Before leaving Paraguay I made a courtesy call on President Morinigo to thank him and the Paraguayan government and people for the courteous treatment we personally and as an MCC organization had received, and also to extend thanks for the way in which Paraguay had opened her doors so magnanimously to the Mennonites in their need. He expressed appreciation for my visit, asked questions about the future of our MCC work, and expressed the hope that it would continue.

Dr. John Schmidt and wife Clara came to Asuncion just before Verna and I left for home. John had been appointed acting director of MCC until the newly appointed one, Gerhard Warkentin of California, came a few months later.

Verna and I started our homeward journey on November 8. When we agreed to go to Paraguay, we had arranged with MCC to go to South America by way of the east coast and return by way of the west coast. Since I taught Latin American, as well as U.S., history I wanted to make the trip as educational as possible. We went by river boat to Corrientes, Argentina, and then crossed the Parana River to Resistencia, taking the train from there to Roca Saenz Pena, near which we visited missionary friends, the J. W. Shanks and the Calvin Holdermans. This was the work among the Toba Indians in the Argentine Chaco. From here we went across Argentina by train to Cordoba and Cosquin, where we briefly visited missionaries, Mr.

and Mrs. D. Parke Lantz. From here we continued by train to Mendoza, the fruit country of Argentina, and then up and through the Andes to Santiago, Chile.

After a several-day visit to this famous central valley of elongated Chile, we decided to take the plane to our next destination, Arica, Chile; and again by train to La Paz, Bolivia. But traveling in a few hours from Arica at sea level up over the mountains to a height of some 14,000 or 15,000 feet above sea level was a mistake! The descent on the other side is very little, and even La Paz is between 12,000 and 13,000 feet. We developed terrible cases of altitude sickness (*soroche*).

Arriving in La Paz toward evening some twenty hours after leaving Arica, we went to our hotel and immediately to bed, still too sick to take off our clothes! About midnight I called down to the clerk to ask whether there was anything we could or should do about our illness. With the voice of experience he calmly assured us we would be feeling better by morning. We were—a little! Unfortunately, instead of spending this day seeing points of interest, we had to spend our feeble energy in going up and down the hills of the city from one office to another until we had accumulated eight government stamps and signatures in order to get out of the country!

From La Paz we crossed beautiful Lake Titicaca to Puna, Peru, and went from there by train to Cuzco. Cuzco is the center of what was the old flourishing Inca and pre-Inca civilization, just as Lima is the center of the Spanish. A visit to Cuzco means also a side trip to the famous ruins at Machu-Picchu. From Cuzco we went by train and plane to Lima, where we remained several days. Our visit here included a trip up into the mountains over a railroad the building of which was a remarkable feat of construction. We traveled over a similar marvel of railroad construction in Ecuador from Guayaquil to Quito and return.

After Ecuador our sightseeing was at an end, and our attention was now centered on getting home by Christmas. From Guayaquil we traveled by plane to Miami, making brief stops at Cali, Colombia, Panama—where the stop was a little longer while changing planes—and at Kingston, Jamaica. From Miami we went by train to Philadelphia and MCC headquarters at Akron, Pennsylvania, and then on to Goshen, stopping briefly enroute at a few places to visit relatives.

We arrived at Goshen on December 24, grateful to Providence for a safe and profitable journey. We were grateful for something else: that we had a land and home to which to return. May I quote from our book, *Paraguayan Interlude* (to which I refer the reader for more details than I am able to include here):

> We had been on foreign soil before, though for shorter periods, and we had felt the thrill of returning home on those occasions. But this time it meant more than ever, and we could appreciate in a new way those words of Sir Walter Scott:
> "Breathes there the man with soul so dead
> Who never to himself hath said,
> This is my own, my native land?"
> But, arriving home on the day before Christmas, in 1945, we had to think of the millions who at that hour, and for a long time to come, had neither home nor native land which they could claim as their own.

CHAPTER 12
The Post-War Years 1946-1954

Both Verna and I were scheduled to resume our teaching at Goshen College the latter part of January 1946. But MCC officials had informed me before we left Paraguay that they would like to have me report to the MCC annual meeting in Chicago, which always met the latter part of December. This was the chief reason we had to leave Asuncion as early as we did. I was happy to give the report at Chicago, and enjoyed meeting many old friends, including students from Paraguay whom we had sent to the U.S. a year earlier.

As Verna and I resumed our teaching at Goshen College we were struck with the changing character of the student body with regard to the various branches of Mennonites represented. Especially was this true of those branches in which the so-called Russian Mennonites constituted important elements. We of course had a few before World War II, but many more after that conflict. In my judgment, the period of W.W. II was something of a watershed in Mennonite history. These years brought significant changes among Mennonites. With so much intermingling among young and older people in Civilian Public Service camps and in the enlarged—especially relief—work of the MCC, Mennonites would never be the same again. They rediscovered Mennonites and Mennonitism. Through this intermingling they also became aware of the various Mennonite colleges, and substantial numbers began to enroll in these newly-discovered institutions. So after W.W. II at Goshen College, in addition to the usual Swiss Mennonite names, we found many such as Penner, Friesen, Buller, Toews, Dyck, Quiring, Peters, De Fehr, Wiebe, Klassen, Reimer, Rempel,

Redekop. These names struck us partly because we had been encountering them in Paraguay.

Another thing that occurred at Goshen after W.W. II was the increase in foreign students. Here too was felt the impact the Mennonites were making on the world through their relief, reconstruction, and other services. That is, frequently foreign students became acquainted with American Mennonite colleges through the college's alumni serving abroad. Some Paraguayan students, for example, came to Goshen because of their acquaintance with Verna and me. A very interesting example occurred in Ethiopia. A person from South India, then living in Ethiopia, happened to meet Orie O. Miller on a train. Orie, an alumnus of Goshen College, was then executive secretary of MCC and also on the Eastern Mennonite Board of Missions. The person from India told Orie about his hope to go to the U.S. to study and was wondering where to go. After some discussion, Orie recommended Goshen where his brother Ernest was then president. Paul Verghese followed Orie's suggestion and graduated from Goshen College with an excellent record.

During the post-W.W. II period student enrollment at Goshen College increased considerably. Along with it the number of our history majors increased, as did also the number of history course offerings. We have always had some excellent history students, but the number of very able ones increased considerably during this period. My favorite teaching courses were naturally those in American history: the survey course, "Economic History of the U.S.", "The West in American History", and, especially, "Recent American History". "American Government", which I taught for many years, was a close second in my interests, and, particularly after traveling and living in Paraguay and in Mexico, I enjoyed teaching "Latin

American History". Teaching the history seminar, which I did for some years, was also one of my favorites. I of course did not teach all these subjects every year.

Committee work continued to occupy part of my time. Especially was this true of the Lecture-Music Committee, of which I was chairman. Though I was chairman both before and after the years mentioned in the above chapter title, it probably would be best to depart from my chronological organization and say a few words about the Lecture-Music Series throughout my connection with it. We had had some very good programs earlier, but beginning in 1950 with the completion of the new Union auditorium—which also served as the gymnasium—we could accomodate many more people and thus finance more expensive numbers, including music, which were second to none. We could advertise that it was no longer necessary to go to Chicago or other large cities to hear the best in music; these artists (and lecturers) could be heard right here in Goshen. Some of the oustanding musical attractions we engaged were the following: Roland Hayes (twice), Marian Anderson (twice), Dame Myra Hess, Cleveland Orchestra (four times), Dorothy Maynor, Elizabeth Swarzkopf, Minneapolis Symphony (twice), Nathan Milstein, Detroit Symphony (twice), Jerome Hines (twice), Vienna Choir Boys, Robert Shaw Chorale and Orchestra (three or four times), Trapp Family Singers (twice), Westminster Choir, Rudolph Serkin, Budapest String Quartet, Roger Wagner Chorale, National Symphony Orchestra, St. Olaf Choir, Indianapolis Symphony Orchestra (a number of times), Obernkirchen Children's Choir, and Toronto Symphony. As to lecturers, the following among others appeared on our series: Carl Sandburg (twice), Carlos P. Romulo, Sam Campbell (illustrated, four or five times), Hodding Carter, Julien Bryan (illustrated), Ralph Lapp, Anthony Nutting, Frank Laubach, Clement Attlee, David Schoenbrun, Countess Tolstoy (daughter of Count Tolstoy), Andrew Cordier, and Martin Luther King, Jr. We usually had seven or eight programs during the course of the school year, September to May, with more music numbers than lectures. A fairly typical year's offering were those in 1957-1958: Cleveland Orchestra, Serenaders Male Quartet, Marian Anderson, St. Olaf Choir, Obernkirchen Children's Choir, Julien Bryan (illustrated), Anthony Nutting, and Ralph Lapp. Or 1959-60 when we had Jerome Hines, Richard Ellsasser, Columbus Boy Choir, Martin Luther King, Jr., Andre Migot (illustrated), Robert Shaw Chorale and Orchestra, Clement Attlee, Minneapolis Symphony, and Karl Robinson (illustrated). We always aimed to have a major symphony orchestra on each year's series, but not two of them as we did in 1958-59—the Detroit and Indianapolis.

The Lecture-Music Committee of the faculty shared with me certain basic beliefs about the value of such a series to the college community as well as to the larger community of Michiana. I believed strongly that if our committee would present a top-notch program, and then let the people know about it by proper advertising, they would support it. This the community did. It was easier to make a more expensive, good series pay its own way financially than a poor one. We advertised the series as a "cultural and educational program for the community operated on a non-profit basis as a public service." Not only the Lecture-Music Committee but the entire college administration cooperated to the end of making this program very successful. We all felt that here was one area in which we could make a worthwhile contribution to our community.

Though the chairmanship required a great deal of my time and effort, the rewards were more than adequate recompense. To hear, for example, Roland Hayes sing "Were You There When They Crucified My Lord," or hear Marian Anderson sing "He Holds The Whole World In His Hands," were emotional and spiritual experiences which I shall never forget. To visit these great spirits before and/or after the program—we entertained some of them in our home—were also experiences I shall never forget. Some artists are not known for their humility. But others are. With regard to the great contralto, Fanny Hurst summed it up well: "Marian Anderson has not grown simply great, she has grown great simply."

Among these great spirits were Martin Luther King, Jr. and Carl Sandburg, both of whom were in our home. Sandburg was there and had dinner with us both times he lectured here. I could tell many stories of my personal experiences with him, but summarizing a few must suffice. When I met him at the railroad station the first time he came (1943) he wanted me to walk with him a bit in the Goshen residential area, and then in the business district. He liked the name "Goshen" he said, and then added: "I could write a poem about Goshen." If he ever did, I never saw it. I then asked Sandburg if he wanted to reserve a room at the hotel. "No," he replied, and then added, "if you have a little hole at the college where I could stay until the evening program that would be all I need." I responded we would be glad to have him stay in our home. This was in the afternoon. So we had him for dinner also. After the evening program we had an informal gathering in our home to which the English faculty members and English majors were invited. One student asked Sandburg for his definition of poetry. Sandburg asked whether he wanted a formal definition, or an off-the-cuff answer. "Off-the-cuff," replied the student. Said Sandburg: "It's a mixture of baloney and cheese." The student was taken aback a bit, but I'm sure he learned a great deal about the poet. For that was Sandburg!

The second time he was here (1953) he also had dinner with us and we had ham. I presided at the meeting that evening, and after the program I shook his hand and thanked him for a fine evening of entertainment. And it really was good—informational and entertaining. His response: "Mr. Smith, do you think your wife has some of that good ham left, enough for a good sandwich?" "I think so," I replied, and so we returned home to retrieve a ham sandwich!

Soon after Sandburg was here the first time he sent me an autographed copy of his book, *The People, Yes*, which I prize very highly.

In the summer of 1947 we decided it was time to take our "advanced course" on traveling in the west, northwest, and Canada. Art Smith again accompanied us, as did also Esther Graber. We followed as closely as possible the Mormon and Oregon trails, and also the California trail as far as Soda Springs, (Idaho), where it turned southwestward, and we continued northwestward to the Oregon country. We fortified ourselves with some excellent guidebooks, which we read and followed religiously, including *The Oregon Trail* in the American Guide Series, and Irene D. Paden's *The Wake of the Prairie Schooner*. Both of these indicated where the old trails went and pointed out the historic places for which we should look.

We first proceeded to Nauvoo, Illinois, where the Mormons were virtually chased out in 1846 after the murder of Joseph and Hirum Smith. A substantial number, led by Brigham Young, went to Utah in 1846-1847. These were known as the Church of Jesus

Christ of Latter-Day Saints. But many Mormons refused to follow Young, remained scattered in the Nauvoo community, and later became part of the Reorganized Church of Jesus Christ of Latter-Day Saints, with headquarters in Independence, Missouri. One reason we selected the summer of 1947 for this journey westward was because it was the centennial year of the Mormons' entrance into Salt Lake Valley, which, according to press reports, Utah was planning to celebrate in a big way. As a professor of American history, with special interest in western and recent American history, I thought that a trip like this would readily vitalize my teaching.

After visiting the historic places in Nauvoo we crossed the Mississippi and followed the Mormon Trail in southern Iowa to Council Bluffs, then crossing the Missouri River to Winter Quarters in Florence, a suburb of Omaha. Whatever you can say about the Mormons, they were great organizers. Ahead of the main body of migrants they would send advance guides to lay out the trail, plant some crops, and even construct some shelters for those coming afterward. A few of these—as in Garden Grove, Iowa, for example—developed into towns which still exist today. Interestingly enough, Garden Grove had a Mormon mayor when we passed through in June, 1947. At Winter Quarters the Mormons spent a terrible winter, about 600 (*Nebraska*, Amer. Guide Series, p.246)—many of them children—succumbing to illness. One of the ironies of U.S. history at this point was the fact that Col. S. W. Kearney came among the Mormons and enlisted approximately 500 men (the famous Mormon Battalion) to march them to Santa Fe and then to California to help take these territories from Mexico against which the U.S. had recently declared war. So the Mormons who were trekking westward toward Mexican territory where they hoped to have more freedom to practice their religion (including polygamy) now furnished 500 men to help make that territory American!

From Winter Quarters we followed the Mormon Trail across Nebraska and Wyoming. Near Kearney, Nebraska, the Mormon converged with the Oregon and California Trails, but remained on the north bank of the Platt River with the others on the south. The Mormons did this, it is said, because of their hostile feelings against non-Mormons. But from Fort Laramie they traveled over the same trail. Near Guernsey, Wyoming, are the most remarkable trail ruts that I have seen anywhere. There the wagons of the Mormons, the Oregonians, and the Californians cut ruts over three feet deep in the rock formation over which they passed. I have taken a number of pictures of trail ruts. These are my favorites.

Unfortunately space does not permit the recounting of all the historic places along these trails: such as Ash Hollow, Courthouse Rock, Chimney Rock, Scott's Bluff, Fort Laramie, Register Cliff, Independence Rock, South Pass, Ft. Bridger, and Salt Lake City, but I must say a few words about two or three of them. For many years I had been hearing and reading about the importance of South Pass in the westward migration—how it was popular because the approach to the summit (of the continental divide) was gradual and easy. The trails followed the North Platte River to the mouth of the Sweetwater and then continued along that stream to the pass. In fact I had read so much about it that I resolved that sometime I would like not only to see it but sleep under the stars at South Pass. In 1947 my wish came true. We had a bit of difficulty in finding it, but that simply added excitement to our quest.

Our interest in this segment of the journey had already been raised to a high pitch by events which had occurred a day or two before. Since there was no road along a portion of the Sweetwater, which the immigrants followed, we had to go northwest almost to Lander and then turn southwest to the pass. But this was no problem for us since we wanted to visit, just beyond Lander, the cemetery that contained the grave of Sacagawea (or Sacajawea), the Shoshone Indian, wife of Toussaint Charboneau and guide to the Lewis and Clark Expedition 1804-1806. We not only visited her grave, between those of her two sons—one of whom as a baby she carried along to the Pacific coast and back—but were pleasantly surprised with a bonus experience just after the visit. In a casual conversation with an attendant at a nearby gas station, he asked whether we had seen Rev. Roberts who lived about a mile down the road. "Who was Rev. Roberts?" we asked. "He was the minister who buried Sacagawea," replied the attendant. This excited us no end. I had known there was controversy as to whether Sacagawea was buried in Wyoming or in North Dakota where she was recruited by Lewis and Clark. So of course we had to visit Rev. Roberts, and spent a most pleasant hour with him—and with one of his sons who was then visiting him. Rev. Roberts had come from England in the early 1880s to serve as an Episcopalian missionary to the Shoshones. He said there was no question in his mind that the person he buried a few years after he came was Sacagawea. In 1947 Rev. Roberts, still in good health, was in his nineties.

So this delightful episode put us in a good frame of mind as we turned southwest toward South Pass. Enroute we went through Atlantic City and spent some time in historic South Pass City. This ghost town was once a flourishing gold-mining center, and was also famous as the community which provided the leadership in making Wyoming, as a territory (1869) and state (1890), the first in the U.S. to have equal suffrage for women.

As to South Pass I shall quote from a report which Art made for a South Bend group in November 1947:

> Our historian [Willard H. Smith] stated that it was his ambition for a number of years to sleep out under the stars of South Pass. There is no road over the pass at present, and one must leave the beaten path to find the marker placed there . . . . The suggestion to stay there for the night, miles from a town and over a mile [7550 ft.] in altitude, at first seemed very foolish to me. I knew it would be very cold there so high up and especially at night . . . . Driving around in the area for several hours looking for the marker we came upon a sheep herdsman who gave us . . . instructions as to the exact location of the Pass and the marker. Nearby we met a car of Mormons who had just come from the Pass, and were on their way to Nauvoo to begin the historic trek on July 15. They verified the directions given by the sheep man, so we were now certain to find the Pass.
>
> In less than an hour we were by the marker at the Pass sitting around a sagebrush fire preparing the evening meal. All the while I was sipping the good hot coffee and nibbling at a sandwich I was wondering whether or not anyone ever stayed at such a cold place overnight. The pioneers at least had a covered wagon for shelter. [Actually the pioneers usually went a short distance beyond the Pass for the night.] Of course we had a car, but four couldn't stretch out very well in such small quarters. Dr. Smith and myself cut more

sagebrush. He informed me that we must have a supply to keep a fire going for several hours. I now resigned myself to our fate of being out under the stars at South Pass all night.

When the sky was aglow with twilight our little party was sitting around the sweet-scented camp fire . . . listening to our historian relate the incidents which made South Pass so famous in the westward march . . .. It was then the most convenient pass over the Divide . . .. He told the stories of Dr. Marcus Whitman and Henry Harmon Spalding, early missionaries to the Indians of the Northwest. The wives of these missionaries, Narcissa Whitman and Eliza Spalding, were [probably] the first white women to cross the Pass. Another interesting character who passed this way was a Hoosier by the name of Ezra Meeker. He went this way [by ox team] in 1852 and settled in Washington . . .. In 1906 he drove an oxen team back to Washington D. C. in the interests of [marking] the Oregon Trail . . .. Later Meeker made the trip in a car, then by train, and finally with the airplane. We gathered more sagebrush for more fire. Stories like this went on for hours. The evening was passing too fast. One could almost sense the spirit of the pioneer in the atmosphere about us—the spirit of heroism, faith, and vision. That evening "under the stars at South Pass" I caught a glimpse of that pioneer spirit.

As to the actual "sleeping," candor compels me to admit that this was not one of our more comfortable nights. Esther and Verna started out in the car, I in the car trunk, and Art on the ground "sleeping" on the only folding cot we had with us. This went on for a couple hours. Then Art began to groan every so often: "Bill, I'm cold!" We then did some reshuffling. I went into the car with the girls, and we promoted Art to the car trunk. Early the next morning we prepared and ate breakfast and then resumed our trek, prepared to tell our friends what a wonderful night we spent at South Pass!

The next stop of importance was at Ft. Bridger, where we knew the Mormons—who were celebrating the anniversary by recapitulating the trek from Nauvoo in "covered automobiles"—were going to encamp for the night and give a program. We were ready for them when they came and we took in the whole show. After the formation of their encircled encampment and the eating of supper by the group of 143 men, 3 women, and 2 children—exact duplication of the pioneer group led by Brigham Young—the leaders made some announcements and distributed the mail that had accumulated at Ft. Bridger. At least one letter was for a Willard H. Smith. The eyes of our group popped, and I investigated. Sure enough, it was for me. We had left Ft. Bridger General Delivery as one of our addresses. The letter got mixed in with the Mormon mail. Intrigued by the name Smith announced over the loudspeaker, a number of Mormons came to me and asked whether I was related to the great Joseph. Not to my knowledge, was my polite reply. These Mormons are strong on genealogy and said I had better investigate. In any case, they started calling me Brother Smith!

We of course planned to stop at Salt Lake City where the really big celebration occurred. Every July 24 is Pioneer Day there. But on the 100th anniversary of the coming of the Mormons into Utah the celebration was on an unprecedented scale! The parades and the floats were all magnificent. But for me the highlight was the dedication of "This is the Place" monument. This is a large beautiful monument, sculpted by Mahonri Young, grandson of Brigham, and located at a point on "Big Mountain" where in 1847 Brigham got his first view of Salt Lake Valley and reportedly said "This is the Place." At the unveiling and dedication of this monument we snapped colored slide pictures right and left. My favorite shots were those taken in front of the Donner Plaque: one with Mahonri Young and two grandchildren and a great-grandson of George and Tamsen Donner, and one of Young alone. LeRoy Hafen, historian whom I had met before, introduced me to Young, who said his favorite plaque also was that of the George Donner party struggling and cutting a road over these Wahsatch Mountains the year before, thus saving the Mormons much time and effort in 1847. The Mormons showed their gratefulness and indebtedness by including this plaque in the monument, and had invited these Donner descendants to be present and unveil it. (For the Donner tragedy see Chapter 10.)

From Salt Lake City, which of course was the end of the Mormon Trail, we proceeded north to Idaho to resume our journey on the Oregon Trail along the Snake River and then over to the Columbia River and the site of the old Whitman Mission. The work of Dr. and Mrs. Whitman and of Henry Harmon and Mrs. Spalding in what are now eastern Washington and western Idaho is one that involves patience, persistence, and drama to the highest degree, not only for church historians, but also for those interested in the history of the westward movement. The regrettable murder by Indians of Marcus and Narcissa Whitman in 1847 and the miraculous saving of the lives of Henry and Eliza Spalding are only part of this dramatic story.

Resuming our trek down the Columbia River Valley, we saw again the scenic views we had seen in 1934. For all practical purposes the Oregon Trail ended in the fertile Willamette Valley to which most of the Oregonians were going in the earlier decades. This time, instead of turning south to California, we turned north to British Columbia and returned home by way of the impressive Canadian Rockies and Glacier National Park. Part of the trip through the Canadian Rockies still required some adventure in 1947, unless one shipped his car from Revelstoke to Golden, British Columbia, by train. Our friends in western British Columbia recommended this, telling how bad and dangerous the road was up north around the bend of the Columbia River. But we decided to take the risk. We did not see as many cars that had fallen down the cliffs as our friends said we would, but we saw a few.

The beauty of Fraser Valley was a fitting introduction to the majesty of the Canadian Rockies farther east. The descriptions, that we had heard and read, of the scenic grandeur of these mountains—from Revelstoke and Golden to Lake Louise and Banff—had not been overdone. So it was likewise with the Waterton and Glacier National Parks farther south. From Glacier we traveled south to visit Yellowstone again on the way home. From here on the territory had been covered before—the Big Horn Mountains in Wyoming, the Black Hills and Bad Lands in South Dakota, and Freeman, South Dakota, where we visited old friends from Paraguay days, Dr. and Mrs. John Schmidt. Dr. Schmidt was serving temporarily as a doctor in this community. We visited briefly in Manson, Iowa, where Verna and Esther's sister Elizabeth and husband Chris Stoltzfus lived. We left Art off at Eureka, Illinois, and after staying there for the night with my brother Tim and family, we proceeded on to Goshen.

After eight weeks and 10,000 miles of meaningful travel, we were happy to be home again, with our cups of inspiration full and overflowing, ready to resume our teaching and associated tasks with new enthusiasm. Some of the associated tasks were committee work, which I have mentioned before, and some research and writing, for which a full teaching load did not leave much time. In 1950 we published *Paraguayan Interlude*—Verna writing one important chapter—and in 1952 my *Schuyler Colfax: The Changing Fortunes of a Political Idol* came out. Smaller research projects were writing some articles and book reviews for our professional journals, and contributing articles to such cooperative works as *The Mennonite Encyclopedia*, and the *Dictionary of American History*. By this time also I had become head of the history department and of the social science division. This increased my administrative work some, and decreased my teaching load only a bit. I now frequently taught the history seminar, which I was glad to do.

Any college or university professor worth his salt will try to keep abreast in his field not only by joining his leading professional organizations and reading their periodicals but will attend as many of their annual meetings as possible. Like most members I have not been able to attend all of these meetings, but I feel that my attendance average has been pretty good. I have always found these meetings stimulating.

One meeting deserves special attention. It was the first meeting of Mexican and American historians planned jointly by both groups and met in Monterey, Mexico, in August, 1949. Verna went with me, and I combined attendance at this meeting with two other assignments that MCC had given me. I was asked to visit and speak at two work camps MCC was then operating—one at Gulfport, Mississippi, and one at Cuauhtemoc, Mexico, where thousands of Canadian Mennonites had been living since the early 1920s. Going to Gulfport first, we then proceeded to Cuauhtemoc by way of El Paso, Texas, and Chihuahua (Chih.), some 230 miles south of El Paso and Juarez, and then about 65 or 70 miles west to our destination. We remained here a few days visiting the MCC staff and a few of the Old Colony Mennonites.

Our next objective was Monterrey where the history conference was to be held. It would have been much closer had we been able to go from Chihuahua to Torreon, Saltillo, and Monterrey. But because of the condition of the roads we were advised to return to El Paso and then travel on the American side to Laredo and there cross into Mexico for Monterrey. Mexico had some good paved roads by that time, but many of the others were in pretty bad shape, including some that were graveled. The road from Chihuahua to Cuahutemoc was in this condition. On the return trip we had more than our share of tire trouble. But therein hangs a tale—a tale of U.S.-Mexican friendship and understanding—that should be recounted.

Frieda Shellenberg, a nurse in the MCC unit at Cuahutemoc who had shown us around in the Mennonite colonies, went with us to Chihuahua. After we had traveled some 15 or 20 miles we had a flat tire. So we put on our spare and proceded. Shortly an officer in the Mexican army asked if he could ride with us to Chihuahua. We said he could. But lo and behold, after we had gone another 15 or 20 miles we had another flat and no spare! What to do? The army captain, the embodiment of politeness and courtesy, would not let me do a thing about repairing the tire, but insisted on getting down in the dirt and doing the work himself. But

164

he didn't have much with which to work. So with the aid of an old butcher knife he tried to make out of the two flats one viable tire that would get us to Chihuahua. His progress was quite meager, and I was anything but optimistic. I thought I would hitch a ride to Chihuahua and purchase a new tire. Another possibility was to buy a tire from the few passersby. The captain would stop these people and ask them. Finally, the captain's efforts paid off. A rancher came along who had a new spare of the right size and was willing to sell! When I settled with him, I wanted to pay him some extra. But he insisted on taking only what the tire had cost him, and then added: "If you ever see a Mexican in the U.S. who is in trouble or need, and you can help him, do so; and I shall feel well repaid." What an expression of international friendship, I thought! And another example of the many courtesies we have experienced south of the border—in Mexico and in other parts of Latin America. I, of course, promised the helpful rancher that I would gladly carry out his request. We put the new tire on, pumped it up, and were soon in Chihuahua. If we should ever meet Frieda Shellenberg (now Mrs. Delbert Erb) again, we would have fun talking about this trip. She had warned us before we started that when she travels with someone, she brings bad luck!

For us, going to Monterrey by way of El Paso and Laredo was not wasted time and effort. Both Verna and I have been interested for many years in this middle country where Hispanics meet Anglos—where the two cultures intermingle. Between El Paso and Laredo we followed the Rio Grande as closely as possible, and, even though on the American side, the population was more Hispanic than Anglo.

Some of the topics discussed at the Monterrey conference—with a few sessions held at Saltillo—had to do with this intermingling of cultures. It was evident too that the Mexican historians had not and could not have forgotten the Mexican War, which they felt, with some justification, was a war of aggression and invasion on the part of the U.S. because Polk and many other Americans wanted California, and the disputed territory between the Nueces River and the Rio Grande River that never had been a part of Spanish or Mexican Texas. But despite the strains and stresses remaining from a painful past, the conference no doubt furthered good will between the two countries.

Another stint of significant travel came at the close of this period. For some years Verna and I had been thinking we ought to do some traveling in Europe. We had made arrangements to do this in 1953. When the Council of Mennonite Colleges found out about our plans, it contacted and persuaded us to lead its annual summer tour of students from Mennonite Colleges to Europe that summer. Going and returning by ship, these students traveled for over five weeks by bus in England, Holland, Belgium, France, Switzerland, Italy, Austria, and Germany, and then spent about four weeks in various work camps rendering service to the communities. Verna and I accepted this assignment with the understanding that while the students were in the work camps we could do some traveling to parts not covered by the student tour—such as the ancestral home of Verna's mother in Switzerland, and in Spain. It all worked out very well, even though the ships on which the Council sent the students were not the kind on which Verna and I had planned to travel. But again we enjoyed traveling with the students and found the summer's experience (our only trip to Europe) definitely valuable and educational.

One activity on the campus during the following school year was of special interest to all of us. In the fall of 1953 the administration appointed an ad hoc committee, of which I was chairman, to arrange a program for January 7, 1954, to celebrate the fiftieth anniversary of the moving of Elkhart Institute to Goshen in 1903. January 7 was selected because that was the date on which the Administration Building was dedicated in 1904. We were fortunate in having early-day leaders serve on the program. President Ernest E. Miller gave the invocation and introduced the chairman of the evening, S. F. Coffman, son of J. S. Coffman, one of the founders of Elkhart Institute. Presidents Noah E. Byers and J. E. Hartzler, and I. W. Royer, student at Elkhart and Goshen—also early pastor at College Mennonite Church—gave interesting and significant addresses. Paul E. Witmer spoke the next day (in chapel) on January 8.

We all felt that the occasion was a successful and significant one. As President Miller wrote to those participating in the program: "We at Goshen are not unaware that we owe a great deal to the vision and sacrifice of our forebears in the work here. May occasions such as this bring us closer together, and may our heavenly Father reward you for your part in making our college possible."

CHAPTER 13
Another Interlude — Mexico 1954-1955

By 1954 another sabbatical was due, and again the question arose as to where and how we should spend it. Since MCC was looking for someone to head up its work in Mexico, and since Verna and I were still interested in Latin America—somewhat as a sideline in my case—we investigated this possibility. We thought too that living and serving in Mexico a year would nicely complement our service in Paraguay by getting acquainted with another part of Latin America and another part of the Mennonite brotherhood. In addition, I had been interested in Mexicans and Mexico ever since as a youngster I had lived in South Texas in the winter of 1908-09. This interest increased later when I studied our relations with Mexico, especially the Mexican War. MCC was happy to accept our services.

In August 1954 Verna and I drove down by way of Newton, Kansas, where we conferred, among others, with J. Winfield Fretz, Cornelius Krahn, and Harry Martens, who had already had some contacts with the work there. Knowing that some of the important leaders of the Old Colony Mennonites were none too sympathetic with MCC's efforts to help them, and knowing also that these leaders had been trying hard to secure copies of the German edition of the *Martyr's Mirror*, Fretz, Krahn, and Martens thought it would be a good stroke if we would take as many of these along in our car as we conveniently could. Fortunately, the Mennonite Publishing House at Scottdale, Pennsylvania, still had a few available, and so Verna and I headed toward Mexico with a car full of *Martyr's Mirrors*! We did not know what the officials would say at the El Paso-Juarez Mexican border, but we thought there was nothing like finding out.

While some of the Old Colony Mennonite religous leaders were not too happy to have MCC start a work in their midst, quite a few of the members were. A drought had occurred among them for three or four years, and many were in need. A number of these had been writing to MCC and to Mennonites in U.S. and Canada asking for help. So MCC decided to respond.

At El Paso we met Tina (Katherine) Fehr, a registered nurse from Manitoba who was to accompany us to Cuauhtemoc. David Karber from the state of Washington, my predecessor as director of the MCC in Mexico, returned from Washington briefly to accompany us to Cuauhtemoc and help get us initiated in the work. Since we had a car full of books, Karber and Tina went from El Paso by public transportation. Knowing the problems of bureaucracy, Karber was a little worried about our getting across the border with all those books. Since we had only tourist visas which expired in six months even Mexican officials might have asked why we were coming to Mexico to read 100 volumes of *Martyr's Mirrors* when we could have done that at home! But the officials were very cooperative and waved us on.

Nearly all of the Mennonites in the Cuauhtemoc area—plus a smaller number near Durango—are of the Old Colony group that came from Manitoba and Saskatchewan in the early 1920s. There are also farther north a few Sommerfelders, a few Kleine-Gemeinde and a small number of Holdeman Mennonites, the result of Holdeman missionary effort. In Cuauhtemoc itself a small number of Russian Mennonites, who left Russia in the 1920s, are located. The Old Colony Mennonites are the most conservative among the so-called Russian Mennonites, comparing somewhat to the Old

Order Amish among those stemming from the Swiss and south German Mennonites. We noticed a considerable difference between the Canadian Mennonites of Paraguay and those in Mexico. Though all are conservative, those in Paraguay—consisting of Sommerfelders, Chortitzers, and a few Bergthalers—are a shade less so than those in Mexico. In the 1950s the Old Colony Mennonites did not use trucks and automobiles. They used tractors, but insisted that they be equipped with the steel wheel rims with lugs in order to eliminate their use as transportation.

One of the first responsibilities facing us after arriving in Cuauhtemoc was to look for a more adequate house to serve as an MCC home and center than the one in use at the time. After a few weeks we found that the centrally located house that the MCC had used earlier was available. I forget whether we rented at first, but in any case we bought it shortly. In having the ground surveyed, we discovered that one of the buildings was a foot or so over the line and thus on another man's property. But after consultation with our lawyer and others involved we decided this was not an insurmountable obstacle and went ahead with the purchase. The owner had business enterprises in Cuauhtemoc but lived in Chihuahua, where we went to close the deal. Verna performed yeoman service by translating the document for us. The house served acceptably and became known as "La Casa Menonita."

One of the first trips to investigate our work and field was the most unforgettable. Bill Snyder, MCC assistant executive secretary from the Akron office, accompanied Harold Voth and me. Harold drove the MCC pickup truck. I decided to take a blanket along "just in case." We went north to visit the various Mennonite colonies and groups. It was the rainy season, and it rained, rained, rained! The return trip proved quite venturesome for tenderfeet (or tenderfoots) like Bill and me. Harold was more used to it. The worst came after dark. The bridgeless streams were flooded, and so were the "roads" (by courtesy) at places also. Some times poor Harold would have to get out, wade in the water, and point out to us where to drive. The worst situation was only a few miles from Cuauhtemoc. A stream was over floodstage and flowing rapidly. One car or truck—it belonged to the Holdeman Mennonites—was stuck in the stream, and others including ours were lined up behind it. We waited for hours. We could see in the distance the lights of Cuauhtemoc, but no way of getting there! It was cold. I was glad I had the blanket along, which I shared with Snyder who was not feeling well. There was also a passenger bus waiting in line with some seats unoccupied. Eventually I gave up my blanket to Bill and Harold and went into the bus to see if I could stretch out and sleep a bit. Finally, around four or five in the morning, we heard of another road where the same swollen stream might then be crossable. We tried it, and it worked, getting home by dawn. But what a night (and a trip) to remember!

Fortunately, not all of our work was that difficult or dramatic. As an MCC we tried to serve the Mennonites and the Mexicans. We helped staff a local municipal hospital with a few nurses and an administrator. Erwin Schrag from Freeman, South Dakota, served in this latter capacity. In addition to Tina Fehr, Esther Swartzendruber and Orpha Leatherman served as nurses while we were there, together with a few Mexican nurses and nurse aids. The hospital served both Mexicans and Mennonites. But confidence in its earlier administration and operation had declined, and MCC was trying to restore it. The coming of Tina who spoke Low German, the language of the Mennonites, and readily learned

Spanish, was an important factor in rebuilding confidence. One weekend statistic, soon after we came, was quite remarkable. Of the total of eight or nine patients in the hospital, seven (no Mennonites) were there because of gunshot or stab wounds! Though this was not the end of admissions due to wounds from violence, the hospital census reports did improve with time.

Harold Voth, who married a nurse, Ruth Friesen, was another of our workers. He served in the field of agriculture, doing experimental work and trying to increase agricultural productivity in the Cuauhtemoc area for both Mennonites and Mexicans. One thing which Harold wanted to do—and we encouraged and helped him in the undertaking—was to go to Mexico City for some months and work with the Rockefeller Foundation, which was in Mexico in part to improve its agriculture.

As in Paraguay, Verna and I were busy with running "La Casa Menonita" and the various administrative tasks in connection with the work. She served as matron of the home. We hired a Mennonite girl from one of the colonies to help with housework. The MCC workers usually lived in the center, and the women helped at times with the cooking as they were able. The home also served as a center for occasional social and religious meetings of Mennonites, especially the young people. The General Conference Mennonite church in the city provided church services regularly on Sunday mornings, thus relieving us of responsibility in this area.

About one religious meeting in our home—a prayer meeting—I had mixed and ambivalent feelings. It was held on the same night as a highly advertised fight between a lion and a horned bull that was part of a circus entertainment. The circus feature came later in the evening, so it was possible to attend both meetings. But should I? Since this type of entertainment, like the bull fights, was loved by the Mexicans, and since I felt I should learn as much as possible about Mexican history and "culture," I decided to attend both meetings, although I had a bit of a problem seeing how one prepared me for the other. Verna chose not to go. The crowd was large and noisy—quite different from our small prayer meeting. But lo and behold! I was able to spot another Mennonite in the crowd—our Mennonite minister who was also at the prayer meeting! I could not blame him, of course. Minsters also, I rationalized, had to know what was going on in the world just like history professors did!

Since we had our car there, part of my administrative duties consisted of car trips to the colonies taking Mennonites back and forth to the hospital in necessary cases, or even occasionally to Chihuahua. I usually took care also of the hospital orders for drugs and supplies that had to be secured in Chihuahua. In addition I took care of those needy Mennonites who came to our home for relief supplies, particularly flour, a supply of which we kept in storage at the center.

Among my duties was that of working on the visa problem for MCC workers. Up to that point all of the Americans and Canadians working there had gone under the easily obtainable tourist visas. This was good for six months. If one wanted to remain longer one had to come back to some American border city and get a new one. Mexico was quite liberal in granting these visas, but not in issuing the immigrant visas for more permanent residence and work. These latter were not only harder to secure but also much more expensive. Even so, we were not fully satisfied with our questionable use of the tourist visas and felt we should try to secure the immigrant visas especially for those planning to remain for longer periods. Tina Fehr was in this category, and so we started the process with her. We had a good lawyer in Mexico City recommended to us by the Rockefeller Foundation. This type of problem was included in those I worked on in the capital. The slow movement of the visa application through the bureaucratic maze was quite bewildering; but with the help of our good lawyer the immigrant visa finally came through. We also started the process for others who were planning to stay in Mexico for longer periods.

One development that apparantly grew out of our service in Mexico was a series of work camps in Cuauhtemoc and tours in the country. The initiative must have come from MCC at Akron. In any case MCC asked us to conduct a work camp for Canadian and American young people at Cuauhtemoc for four weeks, and then take a bus tour for fifteen days to see Mexico as far south as the Mexico City area. These young people were largely but not exclusively from the various Mennonite groups. The work done in the camps was beneficial to the community, like repairing and painting public buildings such as schools and the hospital. Included also were classes in teaching English to Mexicans.

The first work camp and tour came in the summer of 1955 near the end of our term of service. These were repeated in 1956 and 1957. A few more tours, without the work camps, were scheduled later. The last, as I recall, was in 1961. This one had an added feature. Provision was made for those who wished to travel in Central America in addition to Mexico. Another feature that was different about the later tours, after the work camp was eliminated, was changing the age limit of those eligible for the tour. Older adults were welcome to join, and quite a few took advantage of the opportunity. After the work camp was eliminated the tour was extended to almost three weeks in Mexico from border to border.

CHAPTER 14
Fulfilling Years 1955-1968

These were indeed fulfilling, satisfying years. During this period my teaching became still more limited to my field of interest, American history, especially American history since the Civil War, and history of the American frontier. I did continue to teach American government until 1963 when Dan Leatherman came to teach political science; but that was no problem because it was closely related to U.S. history and I was well prepared for it, having had enough graduate work in that field for two master's degrees. I also continued to teach Latin American history unil 1966 when Herbert Minnich joined the faculty and took over the course. But that too was no great problem. I had had courses in the subject, and living and traveling in Mexico and auditing some courses in Mexico City College made for more vitalized teaching in the field, as living in Paraguay had done earlier.

These were satisfying, fulfilling years for another reason. The older and more mature a teacher becomes—the more experience he has with life and its complexities—the more dynamic he can make his teaching and the more sure-footed he can be in his positions. He even becomes more confident in knowing his limitations, which all persons share as regards certain aspects of knowledge. Teaching for a while in such subjects as economics, government, and modern European history—in all of which I had offered auxiliary fields in graduate training—broadened my knowledge and experience, and, I think, made me a better teacher in my major area, American history. But it was gratifying, after such broad and broadening experiences, to be able to confine my teaching to my favorite subjects:

U.S. history since the Civil War, history of the American frontier, and the history seminar.

One unusual, shocking event occurred during this period, and it was interesting to observe the reaction on the campus as well as in the country as a whole. This was the assassination of President John F. Kennedy on November 22, 1963. Assassinating presidents was not new in our history, but none had occurred since 1901. So we were shocked—actually stunned—and stared in disbelief when informed. I was on my way to an afternoon class in "Recent American History" when someone reported the news to me. I thought at first he was joking, but soon found he was not. Meeting a class under such conditions was difficult. Mentioning the sad fact was the first order of business, and about the only thing accomplished that day. After a bit of discussion and a moment of silence I dismissed the class. No one would have gotten much—more probably nothing—from a discussion of the topic scheduled for that period. A few days later the college devoted a lengthened chapel period to a memorial service for the martyred president, in which I, with one or two others, had been asked to say something by way of appraising his contribution, insofar as that was possible at that time.

I had voted for Kennedy rather than Nixon in 1960, but had decided only very shortly before the election. While usually Democratic in my position on the issues, I quite often voted Republican, especially for presidents. Some of my friends could not understand why I would vote for those liberal not to say "Communistic" Democrats. In 1964 for example they could not understand why I supported Johnson instead of Goldwater. (It had been reported in the press that an ad hoc group of Indiana college professors was supporting Johnson, and my name was among them). My response was that I supported progressive candidates because I was *opposed* to Communism. As I see history, one of its great lessons is that the surest way of bringing about social, violent revolution is to pay no attention to reform: just sit on the lid and let the cauldron boil—until it explodes and blows everybody skyhigh. This is what happened in France before the Revolution of 1789, in Mexico before the Revolution of 1910-11, and in Russia before the Revolution of 1917. Even the conservative Bismarck saw this a century ago in Germany and made some concessions to social reform. I always thought that the late Walter Lippmann was one of our ablest publicists and commentators. I agreed with him when he said he believed that the wave of the future was not Communism but social reform. Our own William Jennings Bryan, often called a communist or socialist, pioneered in advocating the social reform view and was one of the most important leaders in bringing about the great Progressive Movement from about 1900 to 1920. Franklin Delano Roosevelt further carried the view to fulfillment in the 1930s. Even the Republicans are not ready to do away with most of these reforms today. Since we do pay attention to reform in the interests of bringing about a more just society, I do not expect Communism to take over in this country. But I do anticipate further changes in social reform from time to time.

This period also included travel of some significance, especially in the mid-sixties. Another trip back to beautiful Colorado in 1959 also had meaning and inspiration for us. Verna's sister, Esther, again accompanied us. This trip west was unusual in that we limited it to Colorado (and of course the states in between). As I believe I said before, I think Colorado has more scenic beauty than any other state in the union—and considerable historic interest besides. We toured the state from north to south and east to west. We also accepted the invitation of Walter and Katie Schertz of La Junta to stay with them in their spacious cabin in the mountains northwest of Colorado Springs, near Green Mountain Falls and Woodland Park.

Another trip the following year (1960) was unusual in that it was eastward rather than westward. I am a little bit like Thoreau was who said, ''eastward I go only by force; westward I go free.'' But not exactly, and especially not in this case, for Verna and I were taking our dear Aunt Emma Schertz to places in the East and Northeast that she wanted to see. Uncle Ben had passed on some years before, and for some time she was contemplating and planning the trip. I had a three-week period in the summer when I could be gone. Verna and I helped her pick out places in which we thought she would be interested—Williamsburg, Virginia, to Washington, Philadelphia, New York, New England, Nova Scotia, New Brunswick, and Quebec.

She paid all of our expenses, and part of her pleasure was in picking out and making reservations in good motels. She insisted on Quality Inns where they were available, and they almost always were in that section of U.S. Aunt knew that taking such a journey was a bit of a risk at her age, but was confident we would take good care of her. She stood the trip well and enjoyed it immensely, talking about it frequently. Aunt died the following January (1961). Verna and I were happy that we could add this joy to her life near the close of her pilgrimage.

Another sabbatical came during this period. This time it was different—not like the two years of service in Paraguay in 1944-45, nor like the year in Mexico August 1954 to August 1955. Having long since become convinced that more research was necessary to do justice to William Jennings Bryan, I decided to spend the winter semester and summer of 1963 working on his life. For some time before this I had begun gathering material on him, and, like many other professors, encouraged my history students to do projects on the Commoner. From January to June I worked on the Bryan papers, and others, in the Library of Congress at Washington, and in the summer I researched the Bryan materials in Omaha and Lincoln, Nebraska. In Omaha Bryan was editor of the *World-Herald* for two years in the mid-1890s. But this paper was an important source of information for the other years of his life also. In Lincoln, Bryan's home for many years, I explored the Bryan papers both in the University of Nebraska Library and in the Nebraska State Historical Society Library.

The summer's research also included a trip in August to Laguna Beach, California, then the home of William Jennings Bryan, Jr. For several years I had been having correspondence with him about his father. He was very cooperative and helpful, not only in the conference I had with him, but also in sending me valuable materials, including a large reel of Bryan correspondence which Bryan Junior had given to Occidental College.

Actually this visit with Bryan Junior was a stop on my way to Mexico City where Verna was spending the summer at Pan American University. Each summer the Spanish Department of Indiana University sponsored a study program for college students, mostly from Indiana, which was affiliated with Pan American University. In the summer of 1963 I.U. had asked Verna to be the leader and director of the group of forty-three. So I decided to go down near the end of the term, spend about two weeks there, and return home by train with Verna and the group. I had also gone to California and Mexico by train, traveling through a part of western Mexico—the part between Nogales on the border and Guadalajara—that I had not seen before. Several subsequent events grew out of this research on Bryan. I had intended to write a biography of him even though a half dozen or so had been written soon after he died in 1925. In my judgment they were all either too laudatory or too critical. None was written by a trained historian. But when I got to doing research on Bryan I discovered that a few other historians had had the same ideas I had about Bryan and had already started producing books that would give a much better balanced, objective view of the Commoner. So I decided to change my focus and write some articles on certain phases of his life.

One unusual thing about Bryan that always intrigued me was his conservative religious views as to theology, and his liberal, progressive political and economic views. So my first article was entitled "William Jennings Bryan and the Social Gospel," in which I tried to demonstrate—I think successfully—that he was not a typical evangelical, or Fundamentalist, in that he strongly believed that the social principles of Christianity should be applied to the every-day problems of life—politically, socially, and economically. So I pointed out in this article that Bryan really had more in common with the so-called social gospelers than with the Fundamentalists. In 1964 I was asked to read a paper on "Bryan and the Social Gospel" at the annual meeting of the Organization of American Historians (formerly the Mississippi Valley Historical Association). In 1967 the *Journal of American History* published the article, slightly enlarged. Then in England the editor, O. O. Winther, told me that I had the honor of having had my article edited at the desk where Karl Marx was supposed to have sat when he wrote his works at the British Museum of History!

Historian Paul Glad also honored me by asking permission to include this article in a book of writings on Bryan that he was editing (*William Jennings Bryan: A Profile*).

My writing on Bryan, especially the article on "Bryan and the Social Gospel", attracted the attention of the historians and officials at Bryan College in Dayton, Tennessee. It was here that the famous Scopes Trial on evolution had occurred in 1925, and where a college was built in honor of Bryan. Verna and I had been doing research there in April, 1965. I was invited to deliver the chief address on Founder's Day, March 18, 1967. I chose as my subject, "William Jennings Bryan—Christian Reformer." Though the college is evangelical in its theology, the audience, composed of faculty, students and friends, seemed gratified to learn that the college's namesake was not the narrow, bigoted Fundamentalist which Clarence Darrow, H. L. Mencken, and the authors of the play and movie, "Inherit the Wind," had tried to foist on the world. The college published the address in booklet form.

In the meantime—in the summer of 1964 to be exact—Verna and I took a group of students through Mexico and Guatemala to El Salvador for an eight-week learning experience in third-world cultures. Most of the time—about six weeks—was spent in El Salvador. The Council of Mennonite Colleges sponsored the study, provided six hours of college credit for participants, and characterized the seminar as "the first seminar in international studies." Henry Weaver of Goshen was particularly interested in the seminar and looked upon it as a sort of pilot program for what he instituted later as a Service Study Term in Central America. We were a total of about fifteen, as I recall, enough to fill a Ford Econoline Van and a Ford Station Wagon. We were fortunate in having Robert Yoder with us—an older, more mature student who spoke Spanish fluently, and who served as our able assistant. We arranged courses in Spanish for the students, as well as lectures and field trips in the history and culture of the country. We depended a great deal on Michael Serrano of San Salvador in helping make these arrangements. The students lived in homes of Salvadoreans, thus augmenting their study of the country's language and culture.

Another trip of great significance to Verna and me was the one we took to Central and South America in the summer of 1965. Because we had not seen Paraguay after we left it in late 1945 we decided to visit it twenty years later. But since we were both still interested in Latin America we decided to see again the parts in between also. I had written to our congressmen John Brademas and Edward Tomlinson for letters of introduction to important leaders in Latin America with whom we could have conferences about conditions in their countries. Tomlinson, who had lectured several times on the Goshen College Lecture-Music Series, was an authority on Latin America, as was Congressman Brademas.

We made brief stops in Guatemala City, San Jose, Costa Rica, Panama City, and longer ones in Bogota, Quito, Lima, Santiago, Buenos Aires, Montevideo, and Asuncion; Iguassu Falls, Curitiba, Sao Paulo, Rio de Janeiro, and Brasilia in Brazil, and then home. In many of these places we had friends, quite a few of whom had attended Goshen College. Frequently they insisted we lodge with them, in some cases coming to our hotels where we had already registered, and making arrangements for us to cancel the reservations. Among those who did this were Howard Habeggar and Gerald Stuckey in Bogota, Nelson Litwiller in Montevideo, and Abe Dueck in Curitiba. One of the great fringe benefits of teaching in a place like Goshen is the acquaintance and friendship with people who in their service become scattered over the world. Particularly in Argentina, Uruguay, Brazil, and especially Paraguay did we meet many old friends.

Naturally, we spent more time in Paraguay (eleven days) than in any other country. They welcomed us with open arms at the MCC *Mennoniten Heim* where we stayed while in Asuncion, and which we had helped establish twenty years before. We met old friends and of course many new ones. It was our good fortune that Jacob Reimer, leader of the Menno Colony, was at the Center at the time and would have room to take us along in his car when he returned home in a day or two. This was a delightful prospect, for we had been anxious to try out the new Chaco road about which we had been reading and hearing so much. Reimer took us to the home of Dr. Wilhelm and Frieda Kaethler in Menno with whom we stayed for a day or two while visiting that colony. Wilhelm and Frieda, two of the first four Paraguayan Mennonite students to come to the U.S. to study in Mennonite academies and colleges, were old friends of ours ever since they lived with us in Asuncion in November and December 1944 while waiting for their travel papers. At the conclusion of our visit with them in Menno they took us to the home of Mr. and Mrs. Abe Peters in Fernheim with whom we stayed during our visit there. At that time Abe was the director of agricultural experiment work in the colony.

The progress made by these colonies in twenty years was remarkable. Religiously the change in Menno was more noticeable than in Fernheim. Attitudes toward Sunday school, manner of worship, evangelism, and education had become much more favorable. Economically the notable development in both colonies was more similar. The work of the agricultural experiment station, with which MCC assisted, no doubt accounted for part of this progress. New crops, especially new grasses for grazing cattle and other livestock, and improved strains of livestock, especially beef and dairy cattle, were evident. Dairying had become much more important by 1965. Communication and transportation had also shown striking development, as indicated by the building of the Chaco road. Tractors, trucks, and automobiles, virtually non-existant in the colonies in 1944-45, were now in wide use.

Returning to Asuncion by public bus, we spent a weekend at the Mennonite Center, and then proceeded to "Kilometer 81" east of the capital where Dr. John and Clara Schmidt were operating an institution for lepers. After a day or two of visiting, the Schmidts decided to go with us to Iguassu Falls. In fact, we went with them in their car. From Iguassu we proceeded to the other points in Brazil as listed in the itinerary, and then home.

As to the conferences with important leaders, they were very helpful not only in understanding conditions in these countries, but also in helping us understand better U.S. relations with Latin America, in which I have had a deep interest for many years. Just as we had seen better relations with Latin America flowing from the Good Neighbor policy twenty years before, so now we were seeing good results coming from John F. Kennedy's Alliance For Progress and other policies. We had conferences with important political and business leaders, as well as with our U.S. diplomatic leaders. One of the most interesting conferences came as a surprise and partly by accident. One evening in our Lima hotel while talking with an official of the APRA Party he asked me if I would like to talk with Victor Raul Haya de la Torre, founder of the party. Astounded, I said "Yes. Is that possible?" He thought he could arrange it for us, and did. It required a trip of some five or ten miles out into the country by taxi, but in view of the man's prominence, and due to the fact that I had been reading and teaching about him for years, I thought the cost would be a bargain. And it was. Not because this controversial person gave us so much information, but to see this man in his home and just to be in his magnetic presence was worth a lot. He had been elected president at least once, and probably twice, but was cheated out of the office because his followers did not control the ballot boxes, and the army opposed him because of his reform ideas and his earlier alleged radicalism. But in a sense he was the "power behind the throne," and his *Apristas* were a powerful influence in the congress. We saw one indication of this that evening. Some representatives of an American telephone company had an appointment with Haya just ahead of ours. They were interested in selling their product to the Peruvian Government and felt it necessary to see Haya first!

It is too bad that Haya de la Torre could not have worked more closely with Fernando Belaunde Terry who was then president of Peru. Basically the two men had many similar ideas with regard to reform. But it seems that old prejudices and perhaps personality clashes kept the two apart. Incidentally, we did not see President Belaunde Terry at that time, but did have a good visit with him some years later when he gave a lecture at Goshen College.

Our last major traveling during this period was another tour to the West in the summer of 1967. Sam and Ethel Yoder of Goshen accompanied us, as did our friend Tina Fehr who had gone to Cuauhtemoc, Mexico, with us in August, 1954. But Tina has remained there since, except for vacations, which she has usually spent at her old home near Winkler, Manitoba. She was there on this occasion when we picked her up. We visited two or three days in this almost solidly Mennonite area of Winkler-Altona-Steinbach, and in Winnipeg which has more Mennonite churches than any other city in the world—some twenty-five or thirty.

From Winkler we proceeded to Saskatoon, Saskatchewan, where Tina (and we also) visited her brother. We stopped next in Edmonton, Alberta, to visit friends, including Rudy Wiebe and family. Rudy had taught several years in Goshen College. From Edmonton we went to the beautiful Canadian Rockies: Jasper National Park, Columbia Ice Fields, Banff, Lake Louise and west through the mountains to scenic Fraser Valley in British Columbia. In Yarrow, Yoders and we visited George Friesens, former students at Goshen, while Tina went on to Vancouver to visit relatives. From Vancouver we went to Buscherts Gardens on Vancouver Island, to Victoria, and then returned on the ferry to the U.S. From here we started eastward by way of Mt. Rainier, Glacier and Yellowstone National Parks.

But before we arrived at Yellowstone we had to make a serious detour. About forty miles southeast of Butte a drunk driver crossed the center line, smashed into us, and demolished our car. Fortunately none of us was hurt seriously, even though I looked a mess with a bloody face and shirt from flying glass. Verna in the back seat was hurt the worst with a couple of cracked ribs. State police were slow in coming. A county sheriff came first. He, accompanied by Tina and Ethel, took Verna to a doctor and then to a hospital in Sheridan where she remained for the night. A state policeman took Sam and me back to a town where I arranged for the disposal of our car as junk, and then took us to join Tina and Ethel in a motel in Sheridan. The next afternoon a Farm State Insurance man from Butte came to take us all back to that city where I bought a new Chevrolet Biscayne six-cylinder. We remained in Butte for the night and resumed our journey the next day. Because of her bound chest Verna traveled and breathed with some difficulty, and I had a bruised chest where I had hit the steering wheel, but we were all thankful to God that none was seriously injured. I left Montana with the strong conviction that we needed stronger laws against drinking drivers. The man that ran into us got off scot-free and had no insurance!

After Yellowstone we journeyed eastward to the Black Hills and Badlands in South Dakota, and then on to Mountain Lake, Minnesota, where we visited briefly the Victor Bullers. From there we turned southward to Manson, Iowa, to stop overnight with Chris and Elizabeth Stoltzfus, Verna's sister. Here I learned again that man proposes but God disposes. We had planned to go home to Goshen the next day. But that night I got sicker than the proverbial dog with stomach disorder—apparently from something I had eaten in a restaurant the day before—and I was immobilized! But the next day Tina had to make her plane connection at O'Hare for Mexico, and so Sam and Ethel took her in the car, and Verna and I came home by train a day or two later. Though the ending left something to be desired, the trip as a huge success, and again "a good time was had by all."

CHAPTER 15
Toward Retirement

This autobiography is finally catching up with us. In this chapter we deal with the period in which we are presently living. With me the process toward retirement began in 1968; for Verna a few years later. It was in 1968 when I went on a part-time basis, teaching only one or two of my favorite courses in American history. Theron Schlabach moved further into American history and took it over altogether when I retired from teaching in 1971. A few years later, when Stuart and Shirley Showalter joined the faculty, Shirley taught some of the American history.

I found this gradual retirement from teaching a very satisfactory arrangement. My "Recent American History" was scheduled for the afternoon, so I had plenty of time "to get up in the morning." What more could a "retired" person want? I also had more time now to work on research. But for this I was no longer a slave to schedule. I worked at my own time and pace. For the first time since I was a youngster I felt like a liberated, emancipated person.

This also meant more time for travel, if we wanted to do that. And we did plenty of it in this period. In 1968—liking train travel as well as by car—we took a tour west arranged by the Burlington Travel Bureau. I had traveled over the California Zephyr's scenic route through the Colorado Rockies and the Feather River Canyon through the Sierra-Nevadas, but Verna had not, and I wanted her to see it too. This took us through the famous Moffat Tunnel west of Denver. Completed in 1957, this tunnel, 6.2 miles in length, reduced the distance from Denver to the Pacific coast 173 miles and effectively put Denver and Colorado on a competive transcontinental route. We stopped briefly in Salt Lake City, and then continued to Oroville, California, where we visited the Wallace Millers. From here we proceeded to San Francisco and the National Parks nearby, especially Yosemite, and Sequoia and King's Canyon which we had not seen before. In San Francisco we took a Grey Line tour of the city, and, of course, had to take some more rides on the cable cars.

Traveling north from here via the Southern Pacific we had to settle on seeing Mt. Shasta from the train on a moonlight night. We continued north to Portland, where we changed to the Great Northern's Empire Builder for the journey to Glacier National Park, which, along with Waterton Lakes National Park, we visited for five days. We had been here before—the last time just a year earlier—but Glacier, with its Going-To-The-Sun Highway and other attractions, is one of those places that one can hardly see too often.

From Glacier we continued on the Empire Builder to Chicago, and then home to Goshen. This famous train was appropriately named after James J. Hill, who was not only the chief organizer and builder of the Great Northern Railroad, but also one of the chief builders of the northwest.

The following year (1969) I decided to make a quick trip to Utah for an important historic occasion. Verna did not accompany me—one of the very few times she did not on a western journey. The occasion was the centennial celebration of the completion of the transcontinental railroad May 10, 1869, at Promontory, Utah. I decided that since I did not make it in 1869 I would be there in 1969. My old friend, Dr. Ernst Correll, who with his wife were now retired in Salt Lake City, had invited me to be their guest. Ernst accompanied me to the celebration, and was able to get tickets on the train and buses to Promontory and for reserved seats at the ceremonies. First there were some talks and then the driving of the last spikes, including the gold one by a person playing the part of Leland Stanford. Then the two locomotives came together to symbolize the linking of the first transcontinental railroad in the U.S. that had been in the discussion and planning stages for decades.

But there was one big difference between 1869 and 1969. That was the participation of the Mormons and the Mormon Church in the ceremonies. The year 1869 was still too close to the antagonisms that had developed between the Mormons and the non-Mormons ("Gentiles") over polygamy and the struggle with U.S. over the control of territorial government. By 1969 these antagonisms and struggles had long since been forgotten. Brigham Young, displaced governor of Utah Territory, was not there in 1869, and he probably would not have attended had he been asked. The great difference in attitudes and feelings in 1969 was well illustrated by the participation of the famous Mormon Tabernacle Choir in the ceremonies. I had heard the choir sing several times in the Tabernacle in Salt Lake City and frequently over the radio and T.V. It was a great thrill to hear them now at the centennial celebration at Promontory in 1969. After their rendition of "Come, Come Ye Saints," I told Ernst Correll: "Ernst, it was worth the cost of this trip just to hear the Mormon Choir sing 'Come, Come Ye Saints' in this setting."

In the following year (1970) Alaska was on our minds. Verna and I had talked about Alaska on various occasions. We had often read about the Alaska Highway; we had seen all of the "lower forty-eight;" and Lena and Esther were ready to join us. So July and August 1970 seemed the right time for this venture.

Desiring to take in as much of Canada enroute as possible, we headed north from Goshen through Michigan to Sault Ste. Marie. Here we entered Canada and followed the Canadian Transcontinental Highway to Winnipeg and Calgary, and then headed north to Edmonton, and then northwest to Dawson Creek, British Columbia, where the Alaska Highway begins. Shortly before reaching the Highway we stopped at a garage which specialized in preparing tourist cars as much as possible against damage from flying rocks or stones. This involved putting protective covers on the front lights, a wire mesh screen in front of the radiator, and a heavy rubber cover under the gas tank. Even so we got our windshield nicked and later replaced it. The distance from Dawson Creek to Tok just across the Alaska border is 1,314 miles. For about ninety miles beyond Dawson Creek the road was paved and the balance to Tok was gravel—"good, bad and indifferent." I never liked gravel roads, and I knew we would have about 1200 miles of them. So I felt it was worth a try at least for once. And it was! The scenery is magnificent! We had new tires and had only two punctures—by sharp stones getting caught in the cleats of the tread. From what we had heard of the experiences of others we were willing to settle for two flats!

One motel especially caught our attention at Milepost 463 (from Dawson Creek). It was called "Wiebe's Wilderness Motel and Fishing Camp." We knew that Wiebe was a good Russian Mennonite name. Though it was only midafternoon when we reached this point, we stopped to look around and inquire. When we saw listed on the menu in the restaurant, among others, such things as Borscht and Zweibach our identity problem was solved beyond a doubt. We bought some refreshments and then had a good visit with Mr. Wiebe. He knew about Goshen

College. His sister had attended there a few years earlier.

In Alaska the highlights of our tour included a visit to Barrow and Point Barrow nearby, where we took pictures of the Arctic Ocean at two a.m.; our visit to the great glaciers; our enforced layover at Soldatna where we had broken a piston (but found a good mechanic there to do the job); our visit to Mt. McKinley National Park; our visit to Mahlon Stoltzfuses at Homer (Mahlon attended G.C. and then served as manager of the college bookstore); and our journey home by ship through the Inside Passage to Prince Rupert, British Columbia. All of us were happy that we did not have to look forward to returning over 1200 miles of gravel road. I wouldn't take a $1000 for the experience of traveling over the Alaska Highway; but I wouldn't give a dime for another one!

From Prince Rupert we traveled homeward by way of Jasper National Park, Columbia Ice Fields, Lake Louise, Banff, Waterton, Glacier and Yellowstone National Parks, and the Black Hills. This scenery is so magnificent that I for one cannot imbibe its inspiration too often.

We again stopped at Manson, Iowa, directly enroute, to visit our sister Elizabeth and husband Chris Stoltzfus.

One face we missed upon returning home was that of my good friend and associate, Professor S. A. Yoder. We received the sad news of his passing just before leaving Anchorage for the homeward journey. Sam and I were close in many ways, including our religious views and in our commitment to Christian education as represented by Goshen College. Besides traveling some together (with Ethel), we often conferred with each other. But these consultations had now ended, to be resumed in that better land.

195

In September (1970) Verna and I resumed our last year of teaching. Officially I was scheduled to retire the following spring, since I would reach seventy in October. At my last class in April (1971), my "Recent American History" students, aided by the other history professors, surprised me with a little party in which they presented me an illustrated book on the 1920s, my favorite decade. So I did retire from teaching, but the college wanted Verna and me to lead a Study-Service Trimester (SST) group to Honduras the following winter. Because of our interest in Latin America we were glad to do this, and found the experience rewarding. But we felt we worked harder at this than when teaching full time at G.C. So our retirement actually occurred in 1972.

One reader of my manuscript was surprised that I had written nothing about singing "Home On The Range." Since I sang it quite often, especially to my classes when we were studying the West, perhaps I should include a word about it before "signing off" as teacher. I always thought a great deal of the song, its words and its tune, and I became so closely connected with it on the Goshen College campus that some began to call me "Home On The Range Smith." The copy of the song I bought in the 1930s had these words printed on the bottom of the front page, "President Franklin D. Roosevelt's Favorite Song." That made the piece still better for me, for in those days I was an admirer of F. D. R. Even though I became more critical of Roosevelt after his first two terms, my appreciation of this folk song has continued. This is true despite Allan Lomax's later remark in a public lecture at Goshen College that he regretted he had to disappoint Professor Smith by pointing out that the song was born in a Kansas barroom!

We had no difficulty in finding things to do after retiring from teaching—traveling, writing, housekeeping, et cetera. I continued my research and writing on William Jennings Bryan, especially his religious thought and his connection with Fundamentalism. I published this latter essay, together with previous articles on Bryan that I had written for several learned periodicals, in a book entitled *The Social and Religious Thought of William Jennings Bryan*, brought out by Coronado Press in 1975.

In the meantime, now being "liberated" from slavery to schedules, we were free to travel at various times of the year. In 1973 we spent February in South Carolina, Georgia, and Florida leisurely traveling down the east coast to Key West and then back up the west coast, visiting friends at various places along the way. At Sarasota, the Mennonite mecca, we remained one week, staying at the Hoosier Manor Motel and Hotel in adjoining Bradenton, owned and operated by Agnes Cripe and her family from Goshen. Agnes was one of my earlier history students. From here we went to Gainesville for a few days of research on Bryan, and then home by way of Tuscaloosa, Alabama, where we briefly visited Carolyn and Tom Diener and family.

In August of 1973 we turned in a new direction: Newfoundland and the Maritime Provinces of Canada. We accepted the invitation of Tim and Louella to accompany them to visit their son John, Joann, and the boys in St. John's, Newfoundland, where John was teaching in the University. Since Verna and I had never seen Newfoundland before, we found the prospect exciting. We went by ferry from Sydney, Nova Scotia to Argentia, not too far from St. John's. John was our capable guide to the interesting places in and around the capital. On the return trip we persuaded Tim to take the circle tour up through Gander—whose large, impressive airport reminds one of former days when the place was an important stopping place enroute to Europe. From Gander we continued over a fairly good paved road to Port aux Basques. We were fortunate in getting passage and cabins on the night ferry back to Sydney. From Sydney we returned to Goshen via beautiful Prince Edward Island (it reminds one of Lancaster County, Pennsylvania) and New England.

The readers (assuming there are some!) of this book may think it was hard for us to get enough of Canada, for in the following year (1974) we made a thirty-day coast-to-coast tour of the country by train. For several years we had been hearing and reading about the deal the Canadian National Railroad was advertising. One could travel for thirty days over any or all parts of the line anytime during the period from October to May. At that time the price was $125.00 per person. The Canadian National covers Canada very widely, touching both coasts at several points and numerous areas in between, north and south. We chose the month of October when the fall colors were most brilliant. One of the highlights of the tour was the trip to Churchill on the Hudson Bay. Since the Pullman was not expensive we traveled that class both ways. Departing from and returning to Winnipeg, we traveled two nights and a day each way. On October 15, the day we were in Churchill, it was 10 degrees above zero (F) at two p.m., with a windchill factor still colder. The wheat shippers were loading the last ship for the season, hoping they could get the cargo out before it would freeze in for the winter. We were fortunate in seeing white polar bears which cannot be seen by tourists in summer.

This tour was one of the best travel bargains we ever had. We spent about half the nights in hotels and the rest on the train in Pullmans or comfortable "Dayniter" coaches which at night could be made into beds almost as comfortable as slumber coaches. In this order we traveled from Windsor to Toronto, Winnipeg, Vancouver, Victoria, and returned to Vancouver, Jasper National Park, Winnipeg, Churchill (and returned to Winnipeg), Ottawa, Montreal, Quebec, Gaspe, Halifax, Sydney, and then returned to Montreal, Toronto, and Windsor. Though the emphasis on this tour was not visiting, we did visit a few friends in Vancouver, Winnipeg, and Halifax.

As stated above, I published my book on Bryan in 1975. This year was also the fiftieth anniversary of his death in Dayton, Tennessee, a few days after the close of the Scopes evolution trial in which Bryan participated. This led to further reappraisal of Bryan, and I was asked to give some addresses on the subject "William Jennings Bryan at Dayton: A View Fifty Years Later." Among those who asked me to speak on the subject was President Ted Mercer of Bryan College in Dayton, where I had spoken some years earlier, and where they were now celebrating the fiftieth anniversary of the Scopes trial and of Bryan's death. A large crowd of faculty, students, and friends seemed to appreciate the fact that historians at long last were seeing and presenting Bryan as a social statesman who for decades had been working for reform and social justice—a view quite different from the greatly distorted picture of a narrow-minded bigot left us by Darrow, Mencken, and others.

January and February of the following year (1976) found us traveling again: this time to south Texas and Mexico. Since we had vacationed in Florida a few years earlier, this time we wanted to try south Texas. We went south through Mississippi, then west through Louisiana to Galveston, and then leisurely along the gulf coast to Brownsville, Texas. We stopped off a few days in Corpus Christi, which I had visited as a kid while living in the winter of 1908 in Tuleta not many miles north. What a change in Corpus Christi! Of course there should have been change in sixty-eight years. In the former year one could still see streetcars pulled by horses or mules, the only time, in my recollection, that I had ever seen that. We also visited Paul Conrads who had children studying at G.C. Paul was minister in the Spanish-speaking Mennonite Church in Corpus Christi. We were happy to attend one or two sessions of a conference of the Spanish-speaking Mennonite churches of south Texas being held in Paul's church.

It was at Brownsville that we received the sad news of the passing of Milt's wife, Gertrude, at Maryville, Tennessee. Since the news was late in reaching us, it was impossible to get to Doylestown, Pennsylvania, where she was buried, in time for the funeral. So all we could do was to telephone Milt and visit him later. On my side of the family this was the first break in the circle of siblings and spouses. Three of Verna's sisters had already passed on by that time: Katie in 1928, Mary Zook in 1952, and Anne in 1968.

After a few days in Brownsville and South Padre Island we resumed our journey up the Rio Grande for a visit to Big Bend National Park and then on to Presidio, which is quite often in the news as one of the hottest places in U.S.

Here we parked our car for nearly a week while making a trip via the recently completed Chihuahua Pacific Railway over the Sierra Madre Occidental Mountains to Los Mochis, located (virtually) on the Pacific. Cuauhtemoc, where we lived in 1954-1955, is located on this railroad, which was not completed over the mountains at that time. We stopped a few days in

Cuauhtemoc for a visit with friends and then proceeded to Los Mochis. In terms of observing magnificent scenery on the grand scale, as well as of witnessing fantastic railroad feats, this trip is difficult to equal anywhere. The canyons rival those of the Grand Canyon area in U.S. (See May 1974 *Reader's Digest* for article "The Most Dramatic Train Ride In the Western Hemisphere.")

We returned to Ojinaga early one morning, and crossed the Rio Grande to Presidio for our breakfast. Here we had the interesting experience of talking with three or four Border Patrol officers, eating in the same restaurant, about the huge problem of patrolling the long border between Mexico and U.S. They conceded that it was a losing battle, catching only about one out of four of those who enter illegally. The basic problem, as I see it, is the tremendous growth of population in Mexico as compared with their resources to take care of their people. In my judgment Mexico needs more planned parenthood. Some Mexicans see this. But too many do not.

From Presidio we proceeded northeast to Wichita Falls, Texas, where we briefly visited my nephew Don Smith and family. From there it was on to Goshen, by way of Russellville, Arkansas, where we visited one of my former students Kenneth Walker, and wife. Kenneth is professor of history at the state school there.

Back in Goshen my chief interest—when not traveling or giving an occasional speech—continued to be that of research and writing. After my book on Bryan was published, I was "inveigled" into writing a history of the Illinois Mennonites. Illinois has an active, strong Mennonite Historical and Genealogical Society. This was the group that asked me to write the book and sponsored the project. This required shifting gears in my research, but I was not a total newcomer to the field. Furthermore, my roots were in Illinois, as indicated in Chapter 1, and I still had many relatives and friends there. So I found the project both interesting and rewarding. It was in the fall of 1976 that the society and I agreed on the terms and scope of the project. I charged nothing for my labor, but the society was generous in paying my expenses: the labor of my assistants, travel, subsidy to the publisher (Herald Press, Scottdale, Pennsylvania) and any other necessary cost. Because of the large amount of Mennonite research facilities located on the Goshen College campus—both in the Archives of the Mennonite Church and in the Mennonite Historical Library—much of the research could be done here, thus cutting down on travel costs. We explored the possibility of getting the work included in the series, *Studies In Anabaptist and Mennonite History*, published by the Mennonite Historical Society. The society agreed to this, and the Herald Press was also pleased with the arrangement. Theron Schlabach served as principal editor of this particular volume. Thanks to the aid of able assistants the manuscript was completed and sent to Scottdale in September 1981 and published in March 1983.

In the meantime Verna and I carried out a few additional travel plans—some of them vacational and some not. In October 1977 we went to Eastern Mennonite College where I gave several addresses on William Jennings Bryan and his impact on American life. This was a rewarding experience, partly because Joe and Minnie Graber accompanied us. They were not only our relatives, but close and dear friends. Ever since I had met Joe at Hesston, this close relationship developed naturally. We were kindred spirits.

We were shocked the following January—although there had been warnings earlier—when Joe suffered some strokes and passed on. Weather-wise it was a poor time to die. Northern Indiana had one of its worst snows in history! Thanks to four-wheeled vehicles, we were able to get to the funeral home for the services. But they had to bury the body later when they could get into the cemetery. An appropriate memorial service was held later at the Prairie Street Mennonite Church in Elkhart where Joes attended. It is not necessary to recount here the important place he filled in the missionary work of the church as missionary (with Minnie) in India, then later with the Board at Elkhart.

In the summer of 1978 Verna and I took another train-trip vacation in our favorite American West, as we had done ten years before. This time we went west on what used to be called the Santa Fe and now Amtrack, stopping off at Newton and Wichita to visit a few friends and relatives and to take in a session of the Mennonite World Conference. Our itinerary included additional stops at Grand Canyon, Los Angeles, Vancouver, British Columbia, Lake Louise, Glacier National Park (Hertz car from Lake Louise to Glacier), and then back to Chicago and home.

In 1979 death again entered our family. Mother Smith died June 5, 1979. She had lived in Michigan since 1920, on the farm until 1926 and then in St. Johns the rest of her life. Father had died in 1924. George was too young in 1926 to begin farming, and the rest of us moved to Goshen to complete college. Fortunately mother was an excellent trained nurse and served at the hospital in St. Johns until she retired in the late 1950s. Even after retiring she worked in the Auxiliary for the promotion of the work of the hospital. Reaching the age of 92, she had a good and full life and won the respect of those who knew her. Nothing illustrates this better than the two following tributes to her. When in December 1915 she resigned as head nurse of the Mennonite Sanitarium at La Junta, Colorado, the patients drew up and signed a series of resolutions which indicated their feelings of deep appreciation and thanks for her kindness and devoted, unselfish service in ministering to their needs. Fifty-seven years later—1972—mother was honored as the citizen of the week (August 14 through 20) in St. Johns—a city of about 7,000—for her devoted service to her church, hospital, and community, even in retirement. The citation, posted publicly, concluded: "For her long-standing concern for others and her willingness to participate we're pleased to name Mrs. Elizabeth Smith as our citizen of the week."

Early in 1980, I was surprised and honored by a letter from the Vice-President's House. Joan Mondale said she and Vice-President Mondale were acquiring biographies of former vice-presidents, to be placed in the "Vice Presidents' Library" which they were establishing. Since some historians had recommended my volume on Schuyler Colfax (vice-president under Grant), she wondered whether I would be willing to send them an autographed copy for the collection. I of course was glad to comply. But I was sorry Verna and I could not attend the dedication ceremonies on May 8 to which we were invited.

For celebrating our fiftieth wedding anniversary September 3, 1980, Verna and I decided to honor the occasion on the installment plan. Since Hawaii was the fiftieth state to come into the Union; since it would be the fiftieth state that we visited; and since this was our fiftieth wedding anniversary, what could be a better place and time than to visit it? When we saw that several airlines were advertising very low fares in May we carried out that part of the celebration at that time. Dr. Byron and Lois Bender and family who lived in

Honolulu were also a drawing factor. Lois (Graber) is a niece of Verna. Honolulu and the state are an interesting melting pot and crossroads in the Pacific. On September 3 we had another installment—a dinner for the brothers and sisters. All were there except Elizabeth (Stoltzfus) of Manson, Iowa. She was able to be here on October 19 when we observed the last part of the celebration. The brothers and sisters insisted on putting this on for us without any planning on our part. George and Wilma had already left for Arizona, and Milton and Betty were called to Pennsylvania because of the death of Betty's brother. In addition to the brothers and sisters, and the only aunt (or uncle) still living, Mary Good, the affair included nieces, nephews, and all kinds of cousins. The oldest ones present were Lydia Oyer, 96, and Aunt Mary, 92. The date selected—October 19, the 199th anniversary of Cornwallis's surrender to Washington after a long siege at Yorktown—was not intended to be symbolic of my surrender to Verna after a long siege of courtship!

Another matter of growing interest to Verna and me has been that of setting up at Goshen College a scholarship in American History and Culture, and then an endowed chair in that area. In order to include Verna's interest in things Spanish, we interpret American to include Latin American history and culture. For years we have enjoyed the annuity method of giving. This method becomes more attractive as one grows older, since the interest rate increases with age. Annuities have several advantages: they pay a good rate of return, especially in your later years; you save a great deal of income tax because most of your income is tax free; you get credit for a gift during the year of the contribution; and since you get income from the gift you don't need to be wealthy to make such contributions. We strongly recommend the annuity method and believe more people would use it if they were fully aware of the advantages.

One thing that came into our thinking more seriously in the early 1980s was moving to the Greencroft retirement center. Our health had been quite good for which we are indeed grateful. In 1976 Verna had undergone surgery for the removal of a malignancy in her intestinal tract, but she soon made good recovery. Other problems however developed. By 1981 she was bothered with circulatory problems and dizziness and blackouts. After hospitalization she made a good recovery. But in February 1983 she had a more serious reoccurrence of the problem. In the meantime, I was having prostate difficulties and had to be operated for that. The recovery was slower than I thought it ought to be. So in the spring of 1983 all signs seemed to point to Greencroft. And to Greencroft we went. We had had our reservations in for many years, and that gave us high priority. But reservations don't help if there is no opening. And there is a waiting list of nearly 1,000. But good fortune smiled on us. An unexpected opening in the kind of facilities we wanted occurred early in May 1983. We were able also to dispose of our home in a satisfactory manner.

Moving from our home at 1619 S. Eighth St., Goshen, where we had lived for forty-six years, to much smaller quarters at Greencroft was an ordeal! Gordon Yoder, Dan Kauffman, and others from the college were generous in aiding us, as well as relatives and friends. But where to put the "stuff"? Obviously we had to get rid of most of it. When Greg and Barbara Smucker, who bought our house, decided to buy most of the furniture, we concluded it would not be necessary to have an auction or even garage sale. We sold the few remaining items piece by piece. Those books I had at home and for which I had no space at

Greencroft I took to my office at the college and disposed of most of them there over a period of time.

After completing my *Mennonites in Illinois* in the fall of 1981, I began working on my autobiography, this present work. So now I am having fun writing my *memoirs*, as Will Rogers used to call them. But if this work ever sees the light of day, and if it ever has readers, they will know about this without further explanation.

As to our pictures, several thousand of them Kodachrome slides used with projectors, I should have been more methodical in carefully labeling them at the time taken. Maybe I can still do some of that, but, unfortunately, not nearly all of it—because of lack of memory if not of time.

CHAPTER 16
End of the Trail: Going Home

In 1915 the American sculptor, James Earle Fraser, created "The End of the Trail" for the Panama-Pacific Exposition in San Fransisco. This famous statue depicts a defeated Indian slumped astride his horse which seems to share the rider's feelings of dejection, despondency, and despair that came as a result of the conquest by the white man in the long march across the American continent. Reading the following passage from Marion Manville Pope apparently inspired Fraser's effort: "The trail is lost, the path is hid and winds that blow from out the ages sweep me on to the chill borderland where Time's spent sands engulf lost peoples and lost trails." (Quoted from Wayne Craven, *Sculpture in America*, p. 493.)

Ever since he was a youngster in Minnesota in the 1880s Fraser had associated and sympathized with the Indians. His father had worked for the Milwaukee Railroad as it built westward. The family often moved along with the father in his work, thus providing James many contacts with various Indian groups. Often Indians also visited his grandfather, and James heard many stories of their treatment by the whites. One old Indian trapper bitterly complained that the "Injuns will all be driven into the Pacific Ocean." The thought so impressed Fraser that he would never forget it. In fact, he wrote, "it created a picture in my mind which eventually became 'The End of the Trail.' I liked the Indians and couldn't understand why they were to be pushed into the Pacific." (James Earle Fraser to Harold G. Schutt, past president of the Tulare County Historical Society, August 17, 1953; quoted in *Story of "End of The Trail,"* p. 6, published n.d. by Visalia,

209

California, Chamber of Commerce. I am indebted to Susan Nafziger Bartel of Visalia who sent me the material from the Chamber.)

The purpose of telling this story of "dejection, despondency, and despair" is to contrast it with the tremendous hope that the Christian pilgrim has when he comes to the end of the trail. It is the difference between night and day—between evening and dawn. Another way of depicting the contrast is suggested in the title of a recent book on the Navajos, *No Place To Go*, by Thayer Scudder and others. That title definitely does not apply to the Christian pilgrim. What Robert Frost said about "Home is the place where, when you have to go there, they have to take you in," is still more true of the Christian pilgrim's home at the end of the journey. The Christian travels with confidence and does not worry about a lodging place at nighttime. He made sure and firm reservations when he became a member of God's kingdom.

Home—what a word! If one were to list the dozen most important and meaningful words in the English language he would have to include "home," along with such words as mother, father, heaven, redemption, faith, hope, love, grace—all closely related. But it is "home" we are emphasizing in this concluding chapter at the end of the trail. Hope and heaven, however, will also loom large because home is heaven (or heaven is home) and hope is the connecting link. I well remember a course in German I took at Hesston College under Professor Gustav Enss and the emphasis he said the Germans put on home. They symbolized this emphasis by their tremendous effort to be at their homes at Christmastime and celebrate the day—or days—with their loved ones.

What a tragedy it is, however, for the millions who do not have a home, or who have a poor excuse of a home, or who have one where Christ is not honored. Robert Frost's poem, "The Death of the Hired Man," well illustrates the tragedy of the homeless, just as the life of John Howard Payne, author of "Home Sweet Home," realistically portrays the human being's poignant longing for home. But I am not a determinist. Such conditions do not have to exist. They can be changed and improved. And Christians must do what they can to bring about change, and bring hope to as many as possible. I strongly believe that Christians should be concerned about people not only having a home in heaven, but also about having one, or a better one, on this earth. For me, an orthodox, evangelical faith includes a strong, Christian social concern. Only then—as I understand Matthew 25:31-46 and I Corinthians 13—can the pilgrim have firm reservations in the home at the end of the trail.

The older one becomes—the more mileposts the pilgrim reaches on that trail—the more he thinks of that home at trail's end. I am reminded of a question a preacher once raised on a Sunday morning. "How many of you want to go to heaven?" he asked his audience during the course of his sermon. Everyone raised a hand except a small boy down in front. Noticing this lack of unanimity, the minister asked, "Johnny, don't you want to go to heaven when you die?" "Oh, yes, when I die," replied the youngster. "But I thought you was gettin' up a bus load to go now." This is a natural reaction. When we are young our immediate relatives and other friends are usually all here and we prefer to remain with them. But as we get older and travel farther toward the celestial city, the more our relatives and friends have passed over and the more connections we establish with that better land. And by the time the pilgrim reaches mileposts in the eighties and especially in the nineties, the lights in the

City become beautifully bright and the pull very strong.

This great theme of home-going and the Christian hope has been expressed and emphasized in many ways and places: in song and story, in prose and poetry, in sermons, speeches, and pictures, and of course in the Bible. We know that heaven will be quite different from hell. In his *Inferno*, Dante has these words printed over the entrance to hell: "Those who enter here abandon all hope." I don't know what hell is going to be like—and I don't intend to find out from personal experience!—but without hope and no possibility of redemption, I believe it is going to be "a hell of a place." (I am not using this phrase as profanity.)

How different heaven will be! It will be home, filled with hope, love, joy, peace, and all the other fruits of the Spirit, and all the other good things of life: reunion, wholeness, security, fellowship, relaxation, a sense of belonging, et cetera, et cetera. Minister Del Glick has well stated:

> Home is a place where we feel comfortable and relaxed. No strangeness for any of us when we go home. Home is where we feel we belong . . . . Jesus assures us that . . . heaven will not feel strange . . . . What a delight to flop down on an easy chair or on the family room rug after a busy day. What a relief to settle down beside a glowing fire, throw off your shoes and relax. You're home! You belong!"

Yes indeed, as Pat Terry says in her song of that title, "I am going home where I belong." "There would I find a settled rest, While others go and come; No more a stranger, nor a guest, But like a child at home." (Isaac Watts.)

212

Since death is simply the door through which we pass to this glorious land there is no reason for fear. William Jennings Bryan stated it eloquently: "Death is a narrow star-lit path uniting the partings of yesterday with the reunions of tomorrow." He said it more fully in his grand statement on Immortality, which I believe will go down in history as one of the greatest pieces of prose in the English language:

> If the Father deigns to touch with divine power the cold and pulseless heart of the buried acorn and to make it burst forth from its prison walls, will He leave neglected in the earth the soul of man, made in the image of his Creator? If He stoops to give to the rose bush, whose withered blossoms float upon the autumn breeze, the sweet assurance of another springtime, will He refuse the words of hope to the sons of men when the frosts of winter come? If matter, mute and inanimate, though changed by the forces of nature into a multitude of forms, can never die, will the imperial spirit of man suffer annihilation when it has paid a brief visit like a royal guest to this tenement of clay? No, I am sure that He who, not withstanding His apparent prodigality, created nothing without a purpose, and wasted not a single atom in all His creation, has made provision for a future life in which man's universal longing for immortality will find its realization. I am as sure that we live again as I am sure that we live today.

This view gives the proper perspective of death and life. Dr. Josephine M. Ford, Bible scholar of Notre Dame who has spoken four or five times at Goshen College, well illustrates the point. Some years ago doctors informed her that she was suffering from a terminal disease. The press reported Dr. Ford as responding: "I believe so strongly in the afterlife that death has no dread for me. I look forward to meeting the Lord." A few years ago Roman Catholic Bishop Romeo Blanchett of Joliet, Illinois, announced to his radio listeners his resignation after his doctors informed him he had an incurable illness—Lou Gehrig disease. He added: "A terminal disease is not something that should bring despair . . .. Everybody is terminal from the day he is born. You start to die when you are born. Some of us are told a little more clearly that it is going to come sooner than [to] others . . .. That is a blessing. When the Lord wants us and takes us, we will have an even better life. It should be a cause for joy."

In different but equally powerful language Victor Hugo put it this way: "For half a century I have been writing my thought in prose and verse: history, philosophy, drama, romance, satire, ode and song. I have tried it all. But I feel I have not said the thousandth part of what is in me. When I go to the grave I can say, like many others, 'I have finished my day's work!' But I cannot say, 'I have finished my life.' My day's work will begin the next morning. The tomb is not a blind alley. It is a thoroughfare to the dawn."

So it is dawn: sunrise, light, a new day, and a new beginning, the resurrection morn, which Christian death symbolizes; not sunset, darkness, night, the gloom of the tomb. Even "at evening time it shall be light." One time some Hindus borrowed from the local Christian missionary some pictures illustrating the life of Christ. The natives looked over the pictures, and though they knew little about Christianity, they knew enough about it to sense that something was wrong. They took the set back and asked the missionary whether the pictures were all there—whether that was the way Christ's life and the Christian story ended. The missionary looked over the pictures more carefully and was dismayed to discover that the picture of Christ's resurrection was missing! Indeed, the tomb was not the end.

We sometimes speak of traveling toward the sunset. I once heard Maurice T. Brackbill give his address, "The Glory of the Sunset." It was on the plains of Colorado where the sunsets are most beautiful. But the imagery is not quite adequate. Christian death goes beyond sunset, however beautiful that may be. It goes to a still more beautiful resurrection dawn and sunrise. The song writer, Virgil P. Broch, caught the vision when he wrote "Beyond the Sunset." All four verses are beautiful. We shall take space for only the first: "Beyond the sunset, O blissful morning, When with our Saviour heaven is begun,—Earth's toiling ended, O glorious dawning; Beyond the sunset, when day is done." (Incidentally, Christian burial tradition supports this view. Christians are buried facing the eastern sunrise, not the western sunset. One funeral director, Robert Ehret, says the tradition is based on Matthew 24:27, which speaks of lightning coming from the east just as the Son of Man will.)

In many, many other songs, also, the theme of our heavenly home has been picked up and sung by millions marching to Zion. One of my favorites is Phoebe Cary's "One Sweetly Solemn Thought." I suppose one reason it is a favorite is the memory, as a youngster, of hearing Elsie Baker sing it so beautifully, time and time again, on Victor Records. The first verse: "One sweetly solemn thought/ Comes to me o'er and o'er;/ I am nearer home today/ Than I've ever been before./ Nearer my Father's house,/ Where the many mansions be;/ Nearer the great white throne,/ Nearer the crystal sea."

One of my favorite symphonies is Dvorak's "New World," partly because of its Largo movement. And I love the Largo movement not only because of its music founded on Negro melodies from the new world, but because William A. Fisher, one of Dvorak's students, wrote the words of "Goin' Home" and set it to the music of the Largo. So that part of the symphony always makes me think of Fisher's words which summarize significantly and meaningfully the Christian pilgrim's home-going at trail's end—not in darkness but in the light of the Morning Star. The first verse follows:

"Goin' home, goin' home, I'm a-goin' home,/ Quiet-like, some still day, I'm jes' goin' home./ It's not far, jes' close by, Through an open door;/ Work all done, care laid by, Gwine to fear no more./ Mother's there, 'spectin' me, Father's waitin' too;/ Lots o' folk gathered there, All the friends I knew,/ All the friends I knew, Home,—I'm goin' home!"

The ultimate and most authoritative affirmation that Christ has conquered death and has gone to prepare a home for us, of course, is the Bible. All of the above that we have been discussing is based on St. Paul's ringing declarations in I Corinthians 15 that "Death is swallowed up in victory . . . thanks . . . to God, who gave us the victory through our Lord Jesus Christ," and his challenging rhetorical questions, "O death, where is thy sting? O grave, where is thy victory?" undergird the Christian hope. In addition, John 14:1-2, and many other Scriptures, give us further assurance that as pilgrims we are traveling toward the heavenly mansions to be welcomed home at the end of the trail by Jesus Christ who prepared them.

So where is this trail leading us, and how far along on that trail are we? As to the second question, only God knows the answer. All that we can say is that we

216

are in the mid-eighties calendar-wise, and also in the years of our lives. According to my own immediate family statistics, I am already living on borrowed time. I still have work to do, but as to what extent I shall be able to complete it is in the hands of God.

But we have assurance on the answer to the first question: Where is the trail leading us? As the title of this memoir states, it is leading us to "holy faith," and thus leading us "home where we belong." And what is the faith to which I was led? I can state it here only in summary. I am an Anabaptist, evangelical, Mennonite Christian. But these terms need clarification. I stem from the peace Anabaptists. I am also a pacifist evangelical with a social conscience, not the militaristic kind without a social concern. I am also a Mennonite who believes in the simple, non-conformed life. Non-conformity was overdone and misinterpreted in its day. But now there is a danger of its passing out and being forgotten. I think the above formula would be a good one for bringing together all Mennonites—indeed all Christians—thus realizing the prayer of Jesus in John 17 that they all may be one.

Traveling along the trail may at times be discouraging. When we look at the world around us and see so many evils that seem to be growing rather than decreasing, we may be tempted to think that instead of "death being swallowed up in victory," good is being swallowed up in evil. The Christian pilgrim may get confused sometimes by the sights along the way. He must keep his perspective with his eyes focused on Christ and the power of His Gospel. I am reminded of a woman in the east who visited her brother, a forest ranger in the western mountains. The brother told her about his work and explained in some detail about the damaging forest fires that they had to fight and for which they had to be constantly looking. During the

217

night the sister was awakened by a brilliant red light coming through her window. She went to awaken her brother and tell him of the fire. When he came to her room to look he explained that the brilliance she saw was not a forest fire but the dawn. He had told her a great deal about forest fires, but had forgotten to tell her about their brilliant dawns! And so it is that sometimes we get the two confused and thus may miss seeing some beautiful dawns!

In closing this chapter, and this memoir, I should like to refer to and quote from two statements on eventide and home-going that have impressed me and with which I can largely identify. One is by Lillian Eichler Watson who wrote about the ninety-fifth birthday celebration of Sir William Mulock, Chief Justice of Ontario. As he stood before the distinguished group that had come to honor him and waited for the applause to subside he mused: "It sounds old. I must seem very old to most of them out there. But strangely enough, I don't feel old at all. It's just another birthday like all the others . . . another year behind me . . . and the best of life still ahead."

This had always been his philosphy, says Ms. Watson. The best of life was always ahead, always farther on—"a philosophy that had served him well, that had kept him young in heart and spirit." "I am still at work, with my hand to the plow, and my face to the future," said the Chief Justice as he began to speak. "The shadows of evening lengthen about me, but morning is in my heart . . . . I have had varied fields of labor, and full contact with men and things, and have warmed both hands before the fire of life." Sir William concluded:

> The testimony I bear is this: that the Castle of Enchantment is not yet behind me. It is before me

still, and daily I catch glimpses of its battlements and towers. The rich spoils of memory are mine. Mine, too, are the precious things of today—books, flowers, pictures, nature, and sport . . . .. The best thing of all is friends. The ~~last~~ best of life is always further on. Its real lure is hidden from our eyes, somewhere behind the hills of time.

To sum it up, Ms. Watson added: "To greet each day without worry or confusion, to do one's appointed task, to be cheerful and unafraid, expectant, responsive—to live simply but fully, enjoying the many great blessings God has provided—that was his message on his ninety-fifth birthday."

The other statement is from Bruce Catton, brilliant writer on the American Civil War. He wrote equally eloquently in his autobiography, *Waiting for the Morning Train—An American Boyhood.* Catton was born and reared in Benzonia, Michigan, near which a small Mennonite congregation existed early in this century, and not far north of Little Eden, the Mennonite Camp at Onekama. The last chapter in his book is entitled "Night Train." Among his boyhood experiences Catton recounts his family's travels by train to visit relatives in Detroit, Chicago, and Minneapolis—how they had to change trains at Thompsonville to take a Pullman sleeper on the Pere Marquette Railroad. Hence the imagery in his book about the morning train and the night train. The last chapter deals with his father's work in later years as superintendent of the Benzonia Christian Academy, and his last illness and death in 1919. The father had abdominal pain—likely cancer—but did his best to ignore it. He finally confided in a doctor, had an operation, and discovered, as he had suspected, that he had incurable cancer.

Catton then reflects on old age. In language that in my judgment reaches such literary heights that it becomes indistinguishable from poetry, he concludes the chapter:

Old age . . . is like youth in this one respect: it finds one waiting at the railroad junction for a train that is never going to come back; and whether the arrival and possible destination of this train is awaited with the high hopes that youth entertains when it waits for its own train depends, no doubt, on the individual. I think Father had hopes.

But you know how it can be, waiting at the junction for the night train. You have seen all of the sights, and it is a little too dark to see any more even if you did miss some, and the waiting room is uncomfortable and the time of waiting is dreary, long-drawn, with a wind from the cold north whipping curls of fog past the green lamps on the switch stands. Finally, far away yet not so far really, the train can be heard; the doctor (or station agent) hears it first, but finally you hear it yourself and you go to the platform to get on. And there is the headlight, shining far down the track, glinting off the steel rails that, like all parallel lines, will meet in infinity, which is after all where the train is going. And there by the steps of the sleeping car is the Pullman conductor, checking off his list. He has your reservation, and he tells you that your berth is all ready for you. And then, he adds the final assurance as you go down the aisle to the curtained bed: 'I'll call you in plenty of time in the morning.' . . . in the morning.

We agree with these statements, with the exception that so far we have found the waiting room neither weary nor long-drawn. Our hands are still to the plow, our faces to the future, and the best of life is still ahead!